MARC CHAGALL

Painter of Dreams

"The Bible has fascinated me

since childhood.

I have always thought of it

as the greatest source of poetry

of all times.

I have sought its reflection

in life and in art."

MARC CHAGALL

MARC CHAGALL

Painter of Dreams

J
759.7
BOBE
c.1

NATALIE S. BOBER

Illustrated by Vera Rosenberry

THE JEWISH PUBLICATION SOCIETY

Philadelphia • New York   5752 / 1991

For

Jody, Melanie, and Joelle

who tripled my joy

by sharing Marc Chagall with me

Library of Congress Cataloging-in-Publication Data
Bober, Natalie.
Marc Chagall : painter of dreams / Natalie S. Bober ;
illustrated by Vera Rosenberry.
— 1st ed.   p.   cm. Includes index.
Summary: Traces the life of the noted painter, from his birth in Russia to
his death in France, with an emphasis on his Jewish background.
ISBN 0–8276–0379–7
1. Chagall, Marc, 1887–1985—Childhood and youth—Juvenile
literature.   2. Artists—Russian S.F.S.R.—Biography—Juvenile
literature.   3. Jews, Russian—Social life and customs—Juvenile
literature. [1. Chagall, Marc, 1887–1985. 2. Artists.   3. Painting,
Russian.   4. Art appreciation.]
I. Rosenberry, Vera, ill.
N6999.C46B6 1991
759.7—dc20   91–25463
[B]   CIP
*   AC*

10 9 8 7 6 5 4 3 2 1

Book design by Adrianne Onderdonk Dudden

CONTENTS

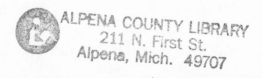

ACKNOWLEDGMENTS

To research a life always requires that we travel many paths and consult varied sources. We must gather the details that breathe life into a human being to help you, the reader, see that person in a particular time and place and understand the forces that shaped his life and his art. I have been most fortunate in my quest.

Numerous fine, scholarly books have been published about Marc Chagall. I have read many of them. Of particular importance were Franz Meyer's monumental monograph, *Marc Chagall*; *Homage to Chagall* and *Chagall in Jerusalem*, published by Leon Amiel; Pierre Provoyeur's book, *Marc Chagall: Biblical Interpretations*; Sidney Alexander's thorough biography of the artist; and Virginia Haggard's story of the seven years she shared with Chagall.

My Life, Chagall's autobiography, and *Burning Lights*, Bella Chagall's tender memoirs, were the source of much information on the early years and of the dialogue. Many quotations come from Chagall's own writing. Ida Chagall graciously allowed me to quote her father's poem, written in his grief at the time of her mother's death.

I have had the help of people happy to share their knowledge of Marc Chagall with me: Jean Bloch Rosensaft, curator of the exhibition *Chagall and the Bible* at the Jewish Museum in 1987, who set me on my course; Terry Trieger; Mrs. Steffler and Mrs. Simont of the Musée National Message Biblique Marc Chagall in Nice; and Perry Silvey, production manager of New York City Ballet, who allowed us to view and photograph all the sets of *Firebird*.

I owe a special debt of gratitude to Rabbi Elkiess of Temple Israélite in Nice and Rabbi Kling, Chief Rabbi of Nice, both of whom spent considerable time conveying to me their recollections of the unhappy circumstances surrounding Chagall's death and burial; Hannah Chinitz, my dedicated emissary to Israel; and Bella Meyer Simonds, who spoke lovingly and sensitively of her special relationship with her grandfather.

My editor, Alice Belgray, offered encouragement, support, and friendship, as well as an astute editorial eye.

Jody and Melanie Lukens–Bober, Betsy Bober Polivy, Pat Lukens, and Sandie Samuels read the manuscript with meticulous attention to detail, offering wise and thoughtful suggestions from their different perspectives.

My husband, whose encouragement and patience seem inexhaustible, accompanied me to France, prodded me to pursue varied avenues of research, offered sage advice, and took hundreds of extraordinary photographs. He makes it all happen.

N.S.B.

Marc Chagall: The Praying Jew (The Rabbi of Vitebsk). *1914, oil on canvas, 46 cm × 35 cm. The Joseph Winterbotham Collection, 1937.188. © 1988 The Art Institute of Chicago, All Rights Reserved.*

Marc Chagall: **The Birthday.** *1915, oil on cardboard, 31¾" × 39¼"*
(80.6 cm × 99.7 cm). Collection, The Museum
of Modern Art, New York. Acquired through the
Lillie P. Bliss Bequest.

Marc Chagall: Green Violinist. *1923–24,*
oil on canvas, 78″ × 42¾″ (198 cm × 108.6 cm).
Solomon R. Guggenheim Museum, New York.
Gift: Solomon R. Guggenheim, 1937.
Photo: David Heald.

Marc Chagall: Bride and Groom with Eiffel Tower. *1938–39,
oil on canvas. Musée National d'Art Moderne,
Centre National d'Art et de Culture Georges Pompidou, Paris.
Photo: Ph. Migeat.*

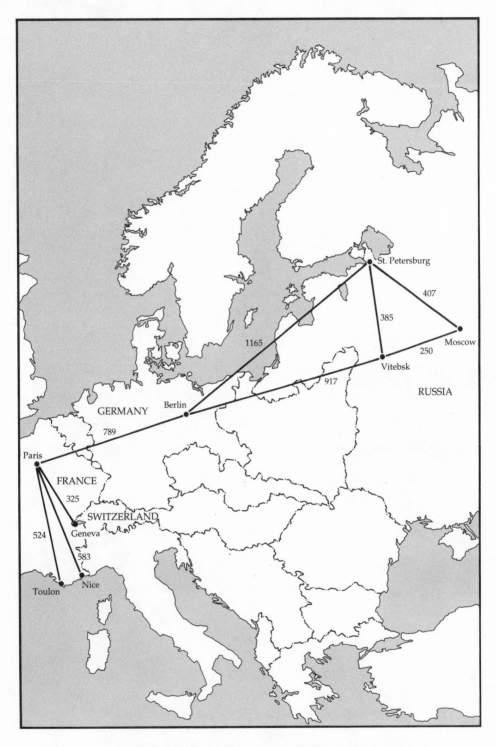

Europe, 1919–1929. Approximate distances between cities (in miles) traveled by Marc Chagall.

MARC CHAGALL

Painter of Dreams

1

"Here Is My Soul"

As a fire raged in the poor Jewish quarter of the tiny village of Pestkowatik in Russia on July 7 in the year 1887, Feiga-Ita Segal, in labor with her first child, was carried on a mattress to the safety of a little wooden cabin across town. But when her baby was born, he appeared to be dead.

Hurriedly, the women who were helping Feiga-Ita pricked the infant with pins, then dunked him into a bucket of water in an attempt to revive him. Finally, after what seemed like an eternity, the baby emitted a feeble whimper. Moishe Segal had come to life.

Soon thereafter, the family moved to the nearby larger town of Vitebsk, to a stone house near the domed church. It was then that Zachar, the infant's father, changed their family name from Segal, a name common among Jews in Russia, to Chagal. Many years later, in

France, his son, by then called Marc, would add the second *l* to make it *sound* French and, perhaps, because *chagall* in Russian means "to stride with big steps."

Vitebsk was a bustling city situated on both sides of the Dvina River in western Russia, near the Lithuanian border. Jews who had been expelled from Moscow settled there, and by 1897, when Marc Chagall was ten, more than half its 65,000 inhabitants were Jewish. The city boasted several synagogues, many houses of prayer, public schools for boys and girls, a Talmud Torah to educate Jewish boys, a rabbinical school, and a Jewish hospital. Jews moved about the city freely.

Synagogues, however, usually built of wood, were forbidden by law to be taller than churches or to be too close to them so that the chanting of prayers might not interfere with Christian services. Some synagogues had beautiful ceremonial objects inside, but many were plain and bare. A few had heavy gates so that Jews might take refuge inside when violent *pogroms*, organized massacres of Jews, suddenly occurred.

The streets of Vitebsk were unpaved, and only about 650 of its 8,000 houses were built of stone. Most were squat timber houses called *isbas*, lined up against a flat, mud-colored landscape. But the city was a rail junction of some importance and therefore a center of light manufacturing. Hundreds of Jewish tailors made clothing to be sold in stores in the large Russian cities. Jews worked in machine shops, linen mills, eyeglass factories, and some were cabinetmakers. Some others were doctors, lawyers, teachers, bankers, and merchants.

Animals were everywhere. Squawking chickens, geese, and ducks strutted about, and cats and dogs,

even goats and cows, roamed freely through the streets, the fields, and the courtyards between houses.

The Chagalls were Hasidic Jews, and little Marc was growing up in the wonder of a Hasidic environment. The essence of the Hasidic religion in Vitebsk at that time was feeling, or emotion, rather than strict observance of law and ritual. The Hasids believed strongly that God and his prophets were present everywhere and in everything. By loving God, Marc's mother explained to him, by faith and belief in prayer, it was possible to work miracles in everyday life.

Sorrow and sadness, she told him, should be banished. Only joyful everyday life would make it possible to properly serve God. So they sang and they danced. And they studied the Bible. Religion was the axle around which their whole existence revolved.

Marc's father, Zachar, was a tall, thin, handsome man with smoldering eyes and the flowing beard of a prophet. But he led the life of a beast of burden and his face was worn with lines and wrinkles. In spite of his Hasidic beliefs he seldom spoke, was always tired, always pensive, always sad.

Zachar was the son of a religious school teacher, a position of great respect in the community and one which earned him a fine living. But for some unknown reason Marc's grandfather decided that his two sons should become workers, one a hairdresser, the other a manual laborer.

So it was that Zachar worked in a herring plant, lifting heavy barrels all day, his boots and shabby clothes wet with brine, his hands frozen from stirring the herring. He earned no more than twenty rubles a month (about 65 cents today). Marc was filled with pity for him. "My heart used to twist like a Turkish bagel as I watched him," he said years later.

Zachar went to synagogue every morning at dawn, then returned home to light the samovar to boil water, drink some sweetened tea, and eat a freshly baked still-warm bun with his family before going off to work. When he returned at the end of the long day, Marc felt that evening entered with his father. As the children clustered around him, he would take from his pockets little cakes and frosted pears that he had brought for them. An evening without them was a sad evening for the children. There were by now eight children, of whom Marc was the eldest. David was Marc's only brother. His six sisters were Aniuta, Zina, Lisa, Manya, Rosa, and Maroussia. (Another sister, Rachel, had died in infancy.)

In shapeless clothes woven at home of thick brown linen, a scarf tied around her head, Marc's mother looked like a nesting Russian peasant doll swollen with petticoats. Always in a hurry, Feiga-Ita managed her household, ordered her husband about, and began to keep a small grocery shop to supplement his meager earnings. Known as a clever businesswoman, she set up her shop herself, stocking it with a wagonload of merchandise, which she was able to purchase on credit, without money.

She was a bright woman who loved to talk and used words well. In the evenings, as the family, filled with food and warmth, sat around the stove after dinner, often all but she and Marc would doze off to sleep. Then she would turn to this oldest, favorite child and say, "My son, I have no one to talk to. You talk to me." But she did the talking, and he listened, rapt, to her fantastic tales.

All week Marc looked forward to the Sabbath. Then Zachar would shed his dirty clothes, take a good wash from the pitcher of hot water Feiga-Ita had brought from the store, and dress in a clean white shirt.

His father's clean hands and face and his white shirt always calmed Marc. When Papa sat down to dinner, everything was all right. The meal, which consisted of stuffed fish, meat with carrots and broth, noodles, calf's-foot jelly, fruit compote, and challah, was always delicious. But it was the custom to serve the meat only to the father.

Later, when Zachar, exhausted from his backbreaking labors, fell asleep with his head on the table, Feiga-Ita would sieze the opportunity to chant the prayers usually sung by the men at the conclusion of the meal and say to her children, "Let us sing the rabbi's song. Help me."

Jewish women were by law and custom subordinate to men and were usually not given religious instruction. Their role was simply to be good mothers and wives, and to leave all dealings with God to their husbands. They were, however, often the ruling force in the home, the core of activity and training of children, and active in business enterprises. They were, in fact, the pulsing heart, the very soul of the family.

Marc's maternal grandfather, Feiga-Ita's father, was a butcher in Lyozno, and Marc loved to visit him there. How he loved him, and how he loved the smell of the tanned cowhides and lambskins that were always hung to dry in his grandfather's rooms.

Often Marc would watch as Grandfather prepared to slaughter a cow. Marc would hug the animal around the neck, whisper good-bye to her, then stand back as the steel blade of the knife plunged into her throat and the red blood streamed out. But he forgave his grandfather this cruelty because he understood that he sold the meat for a living.

One holiday, when Grandfather was visiting at Marc's house, the family suddenly realized that Grandfather had disappeared. They searched all over but they couldn't find him. Finally, Marc discovered him. Grandfather had climbed up on the roof, sat down on one of the chimney pipes, and was happily munching on a carrot while enjoying the fine weather. Marc never forgot this image.

Years later he would paint it—but the grandfather would be holding a fiddle instead of the carrot, a fiddle that reminded Marc of his beloved Uncle Neuch who "played the violin like a cobbler while Grandfather listened dreamily."

It was Uncle Neuch who put on a *tallit* (prayer shawl) every Sabbath and read the Bible aloud while all the children listened. The legends of the Bible were the fairy tales of Marc's childhood. And in the glow of the Sab-

*"Marc soon became an observer at the window,
safely inside looking out."*

bath candles Abraham, Isaac, Jacob, and Joseph, the characters who peopled these fairy tales, seemed to come to life.

Often Marc went into the country with Uncle Neuch to fetch cattle. How happy he was when his uncle agreed to take him along in his jolting cart. On the way home, trying to be helpful, Marc would hold onto the cow's tail, begging it not to lag behind.

This was the atmosphere in which the little boy was growing up. He was a shy, dreamy, timid child with a flashing smile who didn't make friends easily. His cheeks were too pink, his chestnut brown hair too curly. His slanting azure blue eyes and the grace with which he moved made him look almost like a woodland creature. Many of the boys, annoyed by his girlish prettiness, often jumped on him and made fun of him. But he was adored by his mother, his brother David, and his six younger sisters. He was a favorite, also, of his many aunts and uncles, all of whom seemed to feel that there was something special about him. His heart, in turn, overflowed with love for them.

Marc soon became an observer at the window, safely inside looking out. As he watched the outside world from the shelter of his hiding place, it often took on an enchanted quality for him. The street would become a stage, and the townspeople, rabbis, peasants, beggars, fiddlers and other musicians, and the town acrobats became the actors.

Sometimes at night, when everything became calm, he would gaze at the moon and stars from his doorstep on Pokrowskaja Street. Then, as the moon traveled in the sky and the walls of the houses cut off his view, he would climb up on the roof to watch. "Why not?" he asked his mother. "Grandfather climbs up there too."

When he did venture outside during the day, he would wander through the courtyards and alleyways between the *isbas*, among all the squawking animals that would one day file through his pictures in wonderful disguises. And he always carried in his hands a piece of buttered bread "like an eternal symbol."

As he ambled through the noisy, bustling market, he saw barrels of herring, oats, flour, sugar shaped like pointed heads, candles in blue wrappings, and baskets filled with berries, pears, and currants. Peasants moved about restlessly. Roosters for sale cackled, tied up in their baskets. Pigs grunted. Cats meowed. Horses whinnied. And in his mind's eye Marc saw dazzling colors revolving in the sky.

It was a magical world to this dreamy little boy, extraordinarily rich in images. And in the landscape of his imagination, it became for him a world in which it was possible for a fiddler to play on the roof and for cows to jump over the moon. It became part of his memory bank of images from which he would draw all his life. The people, the animals, the wooden houses of Vitebsk, and the surrounding countryside were a world he would eventually leave behind but not abandon, for his roots were deeply embedded in its soil.

"Here is my soul. Here I am. Look for me here," he would say years later.

2

Will I Be an Artist?

For several years before his Bar Mitzvah, Marc attended *cheder*, the elementary religious school where boys were sent to learn enough Hebrew to enable them to read the Holy Books. He was already able to speak Yiddish and Russian. He also studied the Bible and Torah at home with three different rabbis. Every Saturday, instead of going swimming in the river with his friends, he studied Bible with one of the rabbis. He learned to know and love all the characters from the Bible whom he had first met when Uncle Neuch read to him. Now they became real people to him.

For a brief period Marc took singing lessons from a short, stout old man who lived in the same courtyard and violin lessons from Uncle Neuch. Sometimes he sang with the cantor in the synagogue and dreamed of becoming a cantor. Sometimes he thought he would be a dancer or a poet. "Night and day I wrote verses. People spoke well of them." But he was also drawing pictures.

When he reached the age of thirteen, he walked to synagogue with his father, stood on a chair, and recited his prayers in Hebrew. Then he listened and watched as his father, wrapped in his tallit, rocked himself in the rhythm of prayer and recited the principle of the transfer of moral responsibility. Marc had become a Bar Mitzvah, a Son of the Commandments. He was frightened. What did it mean? He wasn't ready to grow up, to leave behind his carefree, protected childhood, to assume responsibility, even to grow a beard. What should I do? he wondered.

Often Marc went to visit his paternal grandfather in Rejitsa. Then he would pass through countryside that was a typical Russian landscape: flat plains, roads bordered with half-wild shrubbery, fields of golden wheat, thick forests of white birch trees, and the Dnieper River, flowing along peacefully.

One Sabbath Marc went to synagogue with his grandfather, as he often did. Marc stood beside him, prayer book in his hands, and gazed out the window. Beneath the drone of prayers the sky suddenly seemed bluer to him, the houses began to float in space, and each passerby stood out clearly. As his grandfather continued to pray, then to chant the melody before the altar, Marc painted a picture in his head of the strange, wondrous things he was seeing.

But it was the Jewish holidays that Marc loved the best. On the High Holidays, before they left for synagogue, his father would find a prayer book for his mother, then show her the pages he had marked: "Begin here; Weep; Listen to the cantor." Then she could be sure that she would cry at the proper places.

One year, on Yom Kippur, the Day of Atonement, the most important day of the year in Jewish life, Marc ran from the synagogue towards a garden hedge, jumped over it, and picked up a large green apple. He knew this was a day on which fasting was required, but he simply had to eat something before evening. He took a bite, then quickly consumed the whole juicy apple, even the core. Only the blue sky saw him. Later, when his mother asked, "Did you fast?" he answered, "Yes." Then he prayed for hours, asking forgiveness.

His favorite holiday was Passover. Nothing excited him as much as the Haggadah, the book read during the seder, which tells the story of how the Israelites were freed from slavery in Egypt long ago. He loved its colored pictures, particularly of the red wine in full glasses. Sometimes the wine in Papa's glass seemed even redder than the pictures. And when his father, raising his wine glass, told Marc to go and open the door for the prophet Elijah, "a cluster of white stars, silvered against the background of the blue velvet sky, forced their way into my eyes and into my heart."

Often Marc even fantasized that Elijah would arrive at his door disguised as a weary beggar. Ultimately he would come to regard Elijah as his own personal protector, believing that it was Elijah's spirit that had revived him when he was born almost dead.

One day, shortly after his Bar Mitzvah, his mother took him to the public elementary school to enroll him. Marc was terrified. He was sure he would be sick to his stomach there, but his mother insisted. When he was refused admission because he was a Jew, Marc thought for a moment he had been saved. But his resourceful and courageous mother walked up to a professor there and offered him fifty rubles to accept her son. The professor, dressed in a uniform of a blue tailcoat with gold buttons, accepted the bribe. Marc entered the third form, because that was the class the professor taught.

When Marc donned the black military uniform and cap of the Russian schoolboy his whole world changed, and he was sad. He knew his lessons, but when the professor called on him he trembled and couldn't recite them. His mouth felt as if it were full of dust. He began to stammer. He had only one thought: "When will I be through with my classes? Will I have to go on much longer? Can't I leave?" He began to concentrate on the girls he could see through the open window. And at home, towards evening, he began to have weeping spells, "as though someone were beating me."

There was one subject he loved, though, and did exceptionally well at: geometry. "Lines, angles, triangles, squares carried me far away to enchanting horizons." And during those hours devoted to drawing he felt like a king.

In his home there were no pictures on the walls. According to the Second Commandment, religious Jews were forbidden to paint: "Thou shalt not make unto thee any graven images, or any likeness of any thing that is in heaven above or that is in the earth beneath or that is in the water beneath the earth."

The Chagalls did have a few photographs of the family, but Marc had never seen a real painting by an artist. Then, one day in his fifth form drawing class, he saw one of his comrades copying an illustration from the magazine *Niwa* onto tissue paper. Suddenly Marc began to tremble. To see this skillful drawing, copied in every detail, was more than he could stand. He knew he had to try the same thing. He ran to the library, asked for an issue of *Niwa*, brought it home, and copied from it a portrait of the composer Anton Rubinstein, showing all the wrinkles and folds in that great man's face. Then he copied other pictures, and his indulgent mother allowed him to pin them up on the walls of his bedroom.

One day soon after, a friend came home from school with him, saw the drawings on the walls, and exclaimed, "I say! You're a real artist, aren't you?"

"An artist!" The word struck like a bolt of lightning. He knew the term, but in his family no one ever pronounced it. "Who's an artist? Is it possible that I, too. . . ?" Marc suddenly remembered that somewhere in the town he had seen a large blue sign,

ARTIST PEN'S SCHOOL OF PAINTING AND DESIGN

and he thought, "I've only to enter that school and I'll be an artist! Now I won't have to be an accountant or a clerk, or a photographer," as his mother had hoped.

A few days later, as his mother was about to put her long-handled bread pan in the oven, Marc came up behind her, took her by her flour-smeared elbow, and said, "Mama, I want to be a painter." Then he continued, "Mama, I can't be a clerk or an accountant. I've had a feeling something was going to happen. I want to be a painter. Save me, Mama. Come with me. There's a place in town. If I'm admitted, and I complete the courses, I'll come out a regular artist. I'd be so happy!"

"What? A painter? You're crazy. Let me put my bread in the oven. Don't bother me. My bread's all ready to bake."

But his mother did consult one of his "modern" uncles, Uncle Pissarevsky, who had read about the important Russian painters. He told her that if Marc had talent, he should try. That settled it. They would go to see artist Pen, and if he thought Marc had talent, his mother would think about it.

So Marc rolled up some of his tattered sketches and, trembling and excited, set out with his mother for the studio of Jehuda Pen. As they climbed the steps Marc found himself surrounded by portraits. The studio, too, was filled with pictures. The walls, even the floors, were covered. Only the ceiling was empty except for giant cobwebs. Marc was intoxicated by the smell of the paints.

When Marc dared to look at his mother, he saw her eyes darting from one to another of the portraits. Then, firmly but sadly, she said to him, "My son, you'll never be able to do things like these. Let's go home."

"Wait, Mama, please."

At just that moment, Pen came in, a short but dignified gentleman with a neatly trimmed blond beard. Jehuda Pen was a "traditional" portrait artist who believed in painting exactly what he saw.

"What can I do for you?" he asked, bowing to Feiga-Ita.

"Well, I don't know . . . he wants to be a painter. . . ."

He's crazy, he is! Please look at his drawings. If he has any talent, it would be worthwhile to take lessons, but if he hasn't . . . Come, my son, we're going home."

But Pen, thumbing through the drawings, mumbled, "Yes, he has some ability. . . ."

That was all Marc needed to hear.

Zachar provided the five rubles necessary for the lessons, but he hurled them into the courtyard for Marc to retrieve. He was almost afraid to permit this sinful undertaking, yet he didn't want to refuse his wife or his son.

When the kindly Pen realized the sacrifice that the parents were making for the son, he offered to charge nothing for the classes. But Marc quickly recognized that while he could learn some technique from Pen, he couldn't learn much else. Pen's way of painting was not Marc's way. Pen's paintings looked like photographs in color. (Photographs then were only black and white.) Marc's paintings were of his own visions: he painted what he imagined, not what he saw. The village was actually mud color. He painted it drenched in color.

And his colors were different, too. Marc had always been intrigued by the color blue: it was the color of the sky, of day, of night. It was even Pen's blue sign that had first attracted him. Still he remained in Pen's class.

When Marc bought a few tubes of paint at the shop next door to Pen's studio and began to use them, he realized that he alone of all the students was using violet. And Pen applauded this courage.

In order to find subjects for his studies that didn't cost money, Marc often went to the outskirts of Vitebsk to paint. As he got nearer to the army camps there, he became frightened and his colors became dingy. But he brought home his paintings of water carriers, little houses, lanterns and processions of people on the hills of Vitebsk, and his mother even hung them on the wall over her bed. Later, though, he noticed that they were gone. His sisters had decided that since the canvases were thick and heavy they would make good carpets for the floors. And another uncle, Great-uncle Israel of Lyozno, on hearing that his nephew drew human figures, was afraid to shake hands with him.

It was at Pen's school that Marc met Victor Mekler, a handsome, dark-haired sensitive young man from a well-to-do Jewish family, whom he had known slightly in elementary school. One day Victor visited Marc at home and asked him to give him art lessons. Marc agreed, but refused any payment. "Let's rather be friends," he said. Victor became his first friend to share his interest in the world of art.

Not long after the two began painting together, Victor made a startling suggestion to his new friend: "Why don't we go to St. Petersburg to study art together?"

Marc was stunned. It had never occurred to him to leave Vitebsk, to leave his family, to leave the world he knew where he was cherished and protected, surrounded with warmth and security. Going to St. Petersburg, he knew, would mean risking poverty and hunger. And Jews of Czarist Russia could not readily leave the Pale of Settlement, the restricted area in which they were allowed to live. A new wave of pogroms had occurred recently, bringing with them the slaughter of hundred of Jews. Jews were now even more limited in their movements. It would not be easy to obtain permission to live in St. Petersburg.

He knew that this city, approximately 350 miles from Vitebsk, and the capital of Russia at that time, was the gathering place for all the new ideas from the West. And there were art schools where he could study. In Vitebsk there was no one except Victor to talk to about art.

Marc had recently been apprenticed to a photographer, where he was learning to retouch photographs, filling in lines and wrinkles to make the subjects look better. The work promised him a good income, but he hated it.

Then, all of a sudden, he thought, "It doesn't matter. With or without money, I'll go. Is it possible that no one, anywhere, will give me a cup of tea, or a piece of bread?" He was terrified, but he knew he couldn't live as he saw his father living. Painting was more important than food.

His art was what mattered, but art that was "different from the painting everyone does." He prayed for the power to paint his vision of life: "God, Thou who hidest in the clouds, or behind the cobbler's house, lay bare my soul, the aching soul of a stammering boy, show me my way. I do not want to be like all the others."

In the end, it was his father who made it possible for Marc to go. Zachar, in spite of his doubts about his son's strange choice of career, obtained the special permit necessary for him to live in St. Petersburg. He persuaded a friend of his, a businessman, to state that Marc was authorized by him to carry goods back and forth between Vitebsk and St. Petersburg. Then Zachar flung twenty-seven rubles, all he could spare, under the table for his son. With tears of gratitude, Marc stooped to pick them up. He understood that this was his father's way of giving.

At the age of nineteen, Marc Chagall, with his almond-shaped sapphire blue eyes, high cheekbones, a mop of chestnut brown curls, and a long, delicate, high-bridged nose, was a slender, graceful young man. Now, shy and self-absorbed, alternately dreamy and intense, but bursting with energy and ambition, he and his friend Victor Meckler set out towards a new life.

3

A Fiddler on the Roof

As soon as he arrived in St. Petersburg, Marc applied to the Baron Stieglitz School of Arts and Crafts. But the entrance examination, which required copying decorative plaster designs, frightened him and he failed. Perhaps, too, his drawings were too personal, too much his own vision. The school wanted a traditional, exact copy. This he couldn't do.

So he enrolled in the school conducted by the Society for the Protection of the Arts, an easier school that did not require an entrance examination. Here he was required to spend most of his time copying plaster heads of ancient Greek and Roman citizens.

In St. Petersburg, Marc knew, the twenty-seven rubles his papa had given him would not last very long. Therefore he found work once again as a retoucher for a photographer. It barely paid for one meager meal a day, however, and he was always hungry. Soon he found himself subject to fainting spells. Finding a place to sleep was a problem, too. Often he shared a tiny room— sometimes just an alcove, once even a bed—with laborers, pushcart vendors, drunkards, even a mysterious Persian.

Eventually, Marc turned for help to Baron David Guinsburg, a wealthy, pious Jew dedicated to helping struggling young Jewish artists. The baron gave Marc an allowance of ten rubles a month for a few months. When that came to an end, another wealthy benefactor, a lawyer and art collector named Goldberg who was allowed to have Jewish servants, befriended him by pretending that Marc was one of the domestic help in his household and allowed him to live there.

Goldberg, who recognized the young man's talent, soon did Marc another service. He introduced him to other art collectors, among them Max Moisevitch Vinaver, one of the leading members of the *duma*, or parliament, who spoke eloquently for political freedom of all Russians, Jews included.

Vinaver was a dignified man with a high forehead and deep-set, penetrating eyes and a neatly trimmed beard. He was a clear thinker who exposed Marc to the works of the Russian Modernist painters. He never failed to ask him, "Well, how are things going?" and seemed to love the poor Jews who were beginning to appear on Marc's canvases. For Marc had already started to put his childhood memories in order and had just painted a stream of pictures of the typical characters he recalled.

One of them was the fiddler, who was then the central figure in Jewish festivities. His plaintive melodies accompanied the basic events of life—births, weddings, funerals—and he became an almost legendary figure in the life pattern of a community. As Marc painted him, with his green face, thumping out the rhythm with his boot on the roof of a tiny wooden house, the fiddler seemed a solitary figure isolated above the village by the strangeness and mystery of his art. Perhaps Marc saw a similarity between his own art and the fiddler's, and this painting became a kind of synonym for Marc Chagall himself.

At the school he was attending, Marc felt he was learning nothing. And the classroom was always cold and damp and smelled of clay, paints, pickled cabbage, and stagnant water from the nearby Moyky Canal. Sometimes his work was praised, and he was even awarded a modest scholarship of ten rubles a month for one year, making it possible for him to treat himself to a daily meal in a little restaurant.

But often, in his still-life class, he was criticized in front of everyone. To his professor his sketches were meaningless daubs. Finally, frustrated, angry, and embarrassed, he left the school, not even bothering to collect his last month's scholarship money. It was July, 1908.

During this time, Marc and Victor had been making occasional trips back to Vitebsk to see their families. Unfortunately, Zachar had been unable to arrange another permit for Marc to travel. After one such trip, Marc was arrested on his way back to St. Petersburg for lacking the special pass required of Jews and for failing to pay the expected bribe. He was thrown into jail for two weeks with thieves and other wrongdoers. He used the time to draw pictures of heads floating around the cells.

After his release, he apprenticed himself to a sign painter in order to qualify for a permit to live in the capital. He had difficulty with the precision necessary to paint the letters, but he loved to see his signs swinging above the entrance to the butcher shop or the fruit shop in the market place. And with his newly acquired permit he could now travel freely back and forth between Vitebsk and St. Petersburg.

But he knew he couldn't go on like this. He wanted to paint. Finally, one day he gathered all his courage, rolled up some of his drawings and carried them to the home of Leon Bakst, who ran an art school that was becoming well known.

Bakst was one of the leaders of a group of artists known as *Mir Iskustvo*, the World of Art. He had recently returned from Paris where he had created sets and costumes for Serge Diaghilev's Ballets Russes troupe (the Russian Ballet). It was Diaghilev who had founded the Russian Ballet in Paris in 1909, and was bringing Western ideas into Russia and taking Russian ideas back to the West.

When Marc arrived at Bakst's home he was told by the maid that the master was still asleep, but he was welcome to wait. It was one o'clock in the afternoon.

Standing in the silent little waiting-room, his drawings clutched in his hands, Marc became more and more agitated as he waited. As he worried about what he would say to the great Bakst, he thought back to the time when he had waited with his mother for Jehuda Pen's approval.

At last Bakst arrived, a kindly Jew with curly reddish hair and a welcoming smile. Marc would never forget that smile.

"What can I do for you?" he asked. Then, "Let me see your studies."

There was no turning back now. Marc picked up his sketches and began to unroll them.

"Yes . . . there's talent here . . . but you've been spoiled. You're on the wrong track," Bakst told him.

There was hope. Marc enrolled in Bakst's school.

The school was different from any Marc had attended. All week long the students would draw or paint from models or from memory. Then, once a week, on Friday, Bakst would appear to criticize their work. One Friday, as the master moved down the long line of canvases, Marc became increasingly anxious. When Bakst finally reached his canvas, he glanced at it, then passed it by without comment. Marc felt humiliated. He gathered his materials and left.

He was certain now that he could learn nothing from

Bakst, or from anyone: "I get nothing except by instinct." So he continued to paint on his own, returning to his original ideas, sorting things out in his mind. Three months later, determined to win the master's approval in front of all the other pupils, he returned, and had the satisfaction of having one of his paintings hung on the wall as a mark of honor.

What Marc did gain from Bakst was the opportunity to listen to the new ideas that were swirling about in St. Petersburg. He heard for the first time of the new traditions, of cubes, of squares, and of Paris, the European capital of art. Marc heard the names of the great innovators—Picasso, Manet, Monet, Matisse, Gauguin, Cézanne, and Van Gogh, the painter who had cut off his ear. And he saw, in reproduction, works by these artists. Later he would describe Bakst as a "breath of Europe."

Marc heard talk, too, of the modern Russian painters' urge to overthrow traditional art concepts, and of the rebirth of imagination in Russian painting. He attended exhibitions that triggered wild debates about modern art. But the young Marc Chagall watched and listened from the sidelines. While others argued, he simply painted, propelled by his own inner vision.

4

"Those Are My Eyes, My Soul"

Through Victor, Marc had been introduced to a circle of well-to-do, intellectual young Jews in Vitebsk who were beginning to break away from the restrictions of Judaism. One was a girl named Thea Brachman, the daughter of a highly respected doctor. Thea had traveled abroad, read French, German, and English, and played the sonatas of Mozart and Beethoven on the piano. Marc liked to be with her. By now he, too, was no longer an observant Jew, although he would never relinquish his strong ties to Judaism.

It was in October, 1909, in Thea's home, on one of his trips back to Vitebsk from St. Petersburg, that Marc first met Bella Rosenfeld, the girl who would become his wife, the love of his life, his guardian angel, his greatest source of inspiration. He was twenty-two years old.

Bella was seventeen. She had just returned from a summer abroad with her mother and was bursting to show her friend Thea her new green cape and hat with a feather to match, unlike anything in Vitebsk, and to share her experiences with her.

The Brachmans lived on a street lined with low stone houses. Their parlor windows, which looked directly onto the street, were hung with heavy drapes to muffle the sounds of the horse-drawn carriages, called *droshkies*, that were driving to the nearby railway station and the clopping of the horses' hooves on the cobblestones.

That day Marc was dozing on the long black oilcloth-covered couch in Dr. Brachman's office while Thea was preparing dinner. He hoped she would come and sit with him when she was finished. After a while he heard someone tapping on the parlor windowpane, then a young girl talking, laughing, almost singing. The sound of her voice was strangely troubling. He had to see who she was.

But when he walked into the cool, dark parlor, filled as it always was with fresh flowers, the girl was already saying good-bye to Thea. She seemed startled at the sight of Marc: his hair tousled as if from sleep, his strange, doe-shaped eyes—the bluest eyes she had ever seen—staring at her. He was laughing. Was he laughing at her? And why was Thea so silent? Why hadn't she told her he was there? Why didn't she introduce them now?

And Marc wondered, Who is she?

"Why are you leaving?" he asked. "What's your hurry? You have such a lovely voice. I heard you laughing."

Bella, Thea, and Marc

The girl didn't answer. She just looked at Thea.

"This is the artist I told you about," Thea said at last.

Marc watched the girl blush, then grab her hat and cape and run out of the house. He didn't know what to make of her. Then, very quickly, Thea suggested they go for a walk to the riverbank. When they got to the bridge over the river, there was the girl, leaning over the railing, alone. Bewildered, unable to comprehend the sudden emotions that were rushing through her, she had stopped running long enough to collect her thoughts, to rest for a moment and enjoy the fresh breeze that was coming up off the river.

Again, Marc was laughing.

Does he laugh all the time, the girl wondered, or is he laughing at me? As they stood there together, not speaking, she noticed that Thea's shoulders drooped and she seemed sad.

Marc's voice broke the stillness: "Let's all go for a walk." Then, "Quick, look over there! That little cloud. First it's pearly gray . . . then dark gray, like steel. Look how it twists and turns." He twisted and turned, too, as if he were trying to catch it. Both he and Bella looked up at the cloud. Suddenly Marc felt as though his feet were no longer touching the ground. He seemed to be soaring over Vitebsk, and Bella was with him.

Marc looked at her—her pale coloring, her enormous round black eyes. He thought, "Those are my eyes, my soul." He knew in that instant that Bella Rosenfeld would be his wife. Suddenly, Thea meant nothing to him.

The next evening Marc walked back to the bridge alone. He loved its wooden planks, the cool breeze that rose up from the water, the scent of flowers that came from the public gardens. It was a refreshing escape from his mother's cramped house.

When he got there, the girl was standing there, watching the waves in the river chasing one another. She seem startled to see him.

"Good evening. Don't be frightened. It's only me." She didn't answer.

"Why are you so scared? Are you out for a walk? So am I. Let's go together." He reached out and took her hand. "Come on, let's get off the bridge and walk along the riverbank. It's beautiful. Nothing to be afraid of. I know. I live there."

Still she said nothing. But she held his hand and went with him. She'd been out a long time and she knew that by now her mother would be worrying about her. She was usually sitting quietly at home on the window seat with her books. What would her family think? But she was strangely drawn to this young man. He seemed strong, "steeped in the strength of the river," she thought.

"What's the matter? Why don't you say something?" Marc asked. "Is it true they call you the Queen of Silence?"

Bella didn't answer.

Marc and Bella began to see each other quietly and secretly. They loved to wander through the town and along the riverbank together. Soon they were sharing their thoughts, their dreams. Eventually, their secret was out. Everyone knew that Bella and Marc were in love, and when Marc asked her to marry him she accepted joyously.

But her family was not happy. The Rosenfelds were one of the wealthiest Jewish families in Vitebsk. Bella's father owned three jewelry shops, and the family lived in a great stone house near the domed cathedral. Their daughter was beautiful and brilliant. She had studied at a fine school for girls in Moscow and had won a gold medal as one of the four best students in Russia. An artist who would never earn a living was certainly not a suitable husband for her.

Marc, too, was well aware of the contrast between the watches and jewels that sparkled in the Rosenfeld's showcases and the herrings of Zachar Chagall. But to Bella, Marc was all that mattered. She loved him, and she knew they belonged together.

Marc continued to travel back and forth between Vitebsk and St. Petersburg. Whenever he returned to Vitebsk he went straight to Bella's house and then to his own. His house was so crowded that it was difficult to find a place where he could paint. Often he climbed on top of the stove in the kitchen to draw, trying not to spill his paints on the newly scrubbed floor.

He was painting Bella. She became a constant source of inspiration for him. His first picture of her, *Portrait of My Fiancée in Black Gloves* (1909), marked a new phase in his work, a turning away from the scenes of his childhood to a more serious, more mature approach.

By 1910 Marc realized that the time had come for him to leave Bakst's school. Bakst himself had already left for Paris to design more sets for Diaghilev's Ballets Russes. Now Marc began to feel as closed in by St. Petersburg as he had by Vitebsk. Even in the larger city he felt stifled. He felt as if he were packed into a herring barrel. He, too, began to dream of Paris, that mythical place to which artists of the East had been traveling for many decades. But how could he go even farther away from his close-knit Hasidic environment to the vast city of Paris, symbol of the western Christian world, where there were bound to be tensions between traditional and new ways of life?

Back in Vitebsk for the summer, Marc begged his father to move the whole family to Paris. Marc would support them.

"What, me go away? And you're the one who's going to feed me? I can just see that!"

"My son, we are your parents," was all his mother would say. "Write to us more often. Ask us for anything you need."

So Marc roamed the streets of Vitebsk and prayed: "God, show me my way. I do not want to be like all the others; I want to see a new world." As if in reply, in his head ". . . the town seemed to snap apart, like the strings of a violin, and all the inhabitants, leaving their usual places, began to walk above the earth. People I knew well settled down on roofs and rested there. All the colors turned upside down."

He made up his mind. "Vitebsk, I'm deserting you. Stay alone with your herrings." He would go to Paris.

It was Max Vinaver who made it possible. Vinaver had great faith in Marc's ability and had already purchased two paintings from him, the first Marc had ever sold. Previously, Marc had taken a pile of canvases to a picture framer in St. Petersburg who offered to try to sell them for him. But when Marc returned a few days later to ask if any had been sold, the proprietor, with an astonished look on his face, said "Pardon me, sir, but who are you? I don't know you." In this way Marc had lost fifty of his canvases.

Now Vinaver offered Marc train fare to Paris and a monthly allowance for him to live there. At the end of August, Marc Chagall once again took leave of his family and his Bella and boarded a train for Paris.

5

City of Light

When Marc arrived in Paris, rumpled, unshaven, and weary after four days in a third-class carriage, he was met by Victor Meckler, who had come to Paris the year before. Marc spent the first few nights sleeping on the floor of Victor's hotel room, then moved to the empty apartment of another Russian friend.

The Paris Marc found when he arrived was very different from Vitebsk and St. Petersburg. Not only was Paris the capital of France, it was considered the artistic and cultural capital of the world. Here artists of diverse backgrounds and talents could pursue a career in an atmosphere free of government control. Even more important for Marc, Jews, who had previously been kept out of the arts altogether, were free to live here as artists *and* as Jews. And within the rich and vibrant environment of Paris, Jewish artists could encourage and nurture one another. No longer would Marc have the constant fear of repression and humiliation. Freedom and equality were taken for granted here.

On the first day after he arrived, Marc hurried to the *Salon des Indépendants*, a large and important art gallery, rushed through all the first rooms, and headed straight to the rooms filled with the French painting of 1910. And there he remained, absorbing all he could of the works of men whose names had previously seemed scarcely more than legends. Now, as he stood in wonder before their pictures, this restless, searching young painter from provincial Russia was overwhelmed. He was seeing for the first time examples of revolutionary movements in art: Cubist, Impressionist, and Fauve.

Daily he made his way on foot to all the galleries and salons that Paris had to offer. Paris was then in the heyday of a cultural revolution that would create "modern art." Artists were experimenting with new ways of seeing and painting.

The timid and raggedy young Chagall was too much in awe of Mr. Vollard, in whose gallery were hung many of the paintings by the new masters, to go inside. He simply pressed his nose against the window to see the unframed pictures that hung on the walls.

As he wandered tirelessly through the city, often munching on a cucumber purchased at one of the markets, he marveled at the light, the *lumière liberté*, a liberating light, as he liked to call it, and lost himself in the teeming life of the streets. Separated from the people as he was by a language barrier—he spoke no French—he could only look and absorb all he saw.

But even as he became more and more enchanted with the work of the French masters, he was searching for something different in his own art. He couldn't help thinking, "Perhaps another eye, another view exists— an eye of another kind and otherwise placed—not there where one is accustomed to find it."

In spite of the wonders of Paris, Marc yearned for Russia, and his family. And he longed to be with Bella. It was only when he visited the Louvre, one of the great art museums of the world, and saw the paintings of the important masters that he began to understand what he had been doing intuitively in his own art, and he was finally able to settle down.

His friend Victor, Marc soon realized, had made little progress in his art and didn't understand Marc's pictures. They began to grow apart. Then, in the summer of 1911, Victor returned to Russia.

In June of that year Marc went backstage during a performance of the Ballets Russes to see Leon Bakst. Bakst was surprised to see his former student, whose talent he had never fully appreciated. But he did offer to visit Marc at his studio, then surprised him by keeping his promise. When he looked at Marc's first Paris paintings Bakst exclaimed, "Now your colors sing!"

That winter Marc moved into a little studio in a strange and startling round building called La Ruche (The Beehive). It was on the outskirts of Paris in a section called Vaugirard. The building was composed of three floors of tiny, dilapidated studios off a central staircase and so really did resemble a beehive.

Here, Marc met other Jewish emigré artists like Jacques Lipchitz and Amedeo Modigliani. He met the

*"Night after night, he painted his fantastic visions
without stop till dawn."*

poet Blaise Cendrars and the brilliant poet and critic Guillaume Apollinaire. And he met the painter Robert Delaunay, who would become one of Marc's few close painter friends. He was introduced into circles where literature, music, and art went hand in hand.

At La Ruche, amid the smell of oil paint that spread through the little cells and the bellowing sounds that came from a nearby slaughterhouse, transporting him back to his childhood, Marc never felt alone. All around him from the other studios he could hear songs, sobs, and arguments. But most of the time Marc chose to remain by himself in his studio.

For he had begun to paint again: "Two, three o'clock in the morning. The sky is blue. Dawn is rising. There, in the distance, they were cutting the throats of the cattle, the cows are lowing and I paint them." Night after night, in a burst of intense creative fever, using his brush like a magic wand, he painted his fantastic visions without stop till dawn: "My lamp burned and I with it." Often he painted on tablecloths, bedsheets, even his shirts torn into pieces, for he had no money for canvases. But if a painting didn't satisfy him, he would hurl it out the window.

An irresistible joy overtook him and he found himself experimenting with bright, intense colors. Color was more important to him even than Cubism, the new art form that was dominating Paris then. After the dull, wintry gray of St. Petersburg, Paris was for him, "light, color, freedom, the sun, the joy of living." The City of Light was giving him a new way of seeing and expressing his familiar material. He felt as though he had been born a second time. Bakst's trembling young student had become an artist who knew exactly what he wanted to do, who had already developed his own style.

His *Paris Through the Window* is considered by many art critics to be the greatest picture of Paris painted in this century. Perhaps more importantly, it seems to evoke a sense of what it felt like to Marc Chagall to be in Paris in 1913, and of the courage it took to launch himself there.

Marc had brought with him to Paris several canvases painted with scenes of Vitebsk, and now he began to rework these, using color to express his feelings. In the glow of memory, as he looked back at Vitebsk through the window of his imagination, he saw it with a Paris sensibility, and he painted a different Vitebsk.

One of the most important paintings that Marc did at this time was *I and the Village,* a joyous, cubist fairy tale of peasants and animals living side by side. It wove his dreamlike memories of Russian folktales, Jewish proverbs, and the Russian village of his childhood into one glowing vision. He was living in Paris, but his Russian roots remained deeply embedded in his soul.

Marc was considered by many of his fellow painters as a strange person with wild ideas, and they often called him *le poète.* In fact, Marc himself was more comfortable with poets than with painters, and throughout his long life he would continue to write lyric poetry. Now the poet Blaise Cendrars, a warm, passionate man who shared Marc's taste for the magical, for dreams, for private worlds, became his closest friend.

Whenever Cendrars came to visit Marc in his studio, Marc would make him wait before he allowed him in. He would hurry to straighten up—to make space amid the messy accumulation of frames, eggshells, empty soup cans, and remnants of herring that were always lying around.

Then this "modern" troubadour would come in, sit down at the open window, and read his latest poems aloud to Marc. Later he would examine Marc's newest paintings. Then, for no particular reason, the two would roar with laughter.

"He looked at my paintings without saying a word, but he was the only one to ever really understand them," Chagall said of Cendrars years later.

But it was the gentle Apollinaire who was the most helpful. As soon as he visited Marc's studio and saw his work, Apollinaire recognized in it a lyric poeticism. He called it *surnaturel* (supernatural). Marc's *Cattle Dealer* particularly made a deep impression on him. Inspired by what he had seen, he wrote a poem to Chagall in which he spoke of his "visit to the round house where a salt herring swims." Later, Apollinaire would write glowing reviews that would call attention to Marc's work. And Marc, in turn, would paint *Homage to Apollinaire*, considered one of his finest pictures of this period.

In March, 1914, Apollinaire introduced Marc to Herwath Walden, the spokesman for the Expressionist art movement then popular in Germany. Walden immediately arranged to exhibit several of Marc's major works in his art gallery, Der Sturm (The Storm), in Berlin. It was at this time that his great painting, *Golgotha*, later renamed *Calvary*, was purchased by a German collector. Then Walden invited Marc to participate in a one-man show at Der Sturm in June.

Marc was elated. By now he was twenty-seven years old, and he was alone in Paris. He had not returned home during the four years he had been there, and he missed Bella. He was beginning to fear that if he remained away any longer he would lose her. He decided that he would attend the opening of the show in Berlin, which was halfway to Vitebsk, then continue on home in time to attend the wedding of one of his sisters, and later, he hoped, his own. He had made up his mind that he must marry Bella now.

He didn't know that nearby guns were being loaded. World War I was about to begin.

6

"She Has Long Been Flying Over My Canvases"

On May 15, confident that he would return to Paris with Bella immediately after the Jewish High Holidays, Marc Chagall simply tied a wire around the lock on his studio door (there was no key), put a huge roll of canvases under his arm, took his cardboard suitcase in hand, and boarded the train for Germany.

In Berlin he delivered all his paintings: forty unframed canvases, the most important he had done in Paris, and about one hundred and sixty gouaches, drawings, and watercolors to the gallery. He saw them simply laid out on tables, then left hurriedly for Vitebsk. He didn't stay long enough to realize that this show would herald his future fame.

Marc's reunion with Bella, who was even more beautiful and sophisticated than he remembered her, was all he had hoped for. Bella had just returned from Moscow where she had completed her studies in history, philosophy, and drama, and she greeted Marc passionately. She, too, was anxious to marry, but her parents still refused to give their consent.

"He will never earn a living. You will perish with him, my child," they told her. "And besides, he's an artist. What will people say?"

Bella didn't answer.

Marc's dream of returning to Paris with a new wife would have to wait. He couldn't marry Bella now, nor could he leave Russia. World War I had broken out and he was stranded in Vitebsk. Once again, his horizons were limited to the narrow provincial life of the little town on the Dvina.

So he rented a tiny studio in an *isba* in the courtyard near his parents' house and settled down at his window to paint "everything that fell under my eye." He was rediscovering Vitebsk. He painted his parents, his brother David playing the mandolin, his sisters, even an old beggar whom he dressed in his father's prayer shawl, then dismissed after half an hour because he smelled too much. But this beggar became *The Praying Jew*, a haunting image and one of the greatest of Marc's paintings. Marc's eyes saw a poor Jew, a common sight in Vitebsk, but his excited imagination drew an epic figure who might have stepped out of the Old Testament. Within one year Marc had painted almost sixty "documents" of Vitebsk of 1914, as he called them, all on cardboard or paper because it was impossible to get canvas.

When good paints also became difficult to obtain, he began to work in another medium: pen and ink. He discovered he possessed a natural gift for illustration. Some of his drawings looked like German woodcuts, and some seemed to echo the illustrations in the ancient Haggadahs. He would use this talent again years later.

But Vitebsk was no longer the same to Marc. After the exhilaration of Paris it was "a strange town, an unhappy town, a boring town." His only happiness came when Bella visited him at his studio, as she often did, bringing with her sweet cakes, boiled milk, broiled fish from her own home, even some boards that Marc made into an easel. And she always brought fresh flowers. Often she came and went through the window. "I had only to open my window and blue air, love and flowers entered with her," Marc said years later. She inspired beautiful, magical paintings.

One warm summer morning Bella wandered through the outskirts of town, gathering tall blue wildflowers to bring to Marc. She knew it was his birthday, and she wanted it to be special. Back at home, she arranged the flowers into a lovely bouquet. Then she gathered some biscuits and fried fish, assembled some scarves of brightly colored silk, and even took the embroidered quilt off her bed. She changed into her best dress and, feeling loaded down "like a donkey," started for Marc's house across town.

"Where is she going, that crazy girl, with so many parcels?" the neighbors wondered as she hurried by.

Finally, she crossed the bridge, then ran along the stream until she reached Marc's cottage. As he opened the shutter to let her slip in, he was astonished.

"Where are you coming from? What do you have?"

"You think with packages one must be coming from the station? Guess, what date is it?"

"Ask me an easier question. I don't even know what day it is."

"Today is your birthday!"

Marc's jaw dropped.

Bella quickly untied her multicolored shawls and hung them on the wall. She stretched one out on the table, and placed her quilt on Marc's cot. She still held the flowers in her hand.

"Don't move! Stay just like that," Marc commanded. He quickly set up his easel and began to paint "so fast that red and blue, black and white flew through the air. They swept me with them," Bella reminisced years later, when she wrote her memoirs. "I suddenly felt as if I were taking off. You, too, were poised on one leg, as if the little room could no longer contain you. You soared up to the ceiling. Your head turned down to mine and turned mine up to you, brushing against my ear and whispering something. Together we floated up above the room with all its finery, and flew," she continued.

Suddenly, they were back on earth again. But on Marc's canvas a simple room had been transformed into a place where miracles could happen.

"What do you think of it?" Marc asked. "Does it need more work?"

"Oh, it's very good! We'll call it *The Birthday*."

"Will you come again tomorrow? I'll paint another picture. And we'll fly away again."

And fly away they did. The determined Bella finally won her parents' consent to their marriage.

On July 25, 1915, a warm, rainy evening, Marc, pale and nervous, found himself at his fiancée's house. Timidly, he made his way through the assembled guests in the flower-bedecked parlor toward the richly embroidered red silk *chuppa*, the canopy under which a Jewish wedding ceremony takes place. As the Rosenfeld and Chagall families eyed each other icily from opposite sides of the room, Marc caught snatches of their conversations: "An artist . . ."; ". . . gets money for his pictures . . ."; ". . . no way to earn a living . . ."; "Who is his father?"

Then, as the chief rabbi of Vitebsk pronounced the age-old blessings that united Marc and Bella in marriage, Marc was overcome with emotion. As he stood with his bride, listening to the rabbi's words, he pressed her delicate, fine-boned hand, longing to flee with her to the country, to embrace her, to laugh with her.

The image of their wedding would stay with Marc always. It would find its way into many paintings in which bride and groom embraced in clouds or among flowers, sometimes even upside down—like Marc and Bella.

When the newlyweds finally escaped for a honeymoon in the countryside outside Vitebsk, Marc called it a "milkmoon." Every morning cowherds from the Russian army passing nearby illegally sold them pailfuls of milk for a few kopeks, less than a penny's worth today. By autumn Marc had gained so much weight that he could scarcely button his jacket. For a short time they were even able to forget that there was a war going on.

Often, when Marc and Bella returned from an evening walk, they would sit down at a table and write messages to one another expressing feelings they couldn't speak aloud. In spite of their families' objections and concerns, their marriage blossomed into a moving and passionate love story. Bella became the love of Marc's life. Her keen intelligence and her poetic and sensitive nature were in perfect harmony with his. Subtle, patient, determined, she understood her husband and his needs. She offered him affection, protection, and the shelter out of which he could look at the world in his own fashion and paint it as he saw it. Bella became a crucial source of ideas for him and the one critic whose advice he always followed.

Marc, aware of Bella's sacrifice in marrying a young man so far beneath her social status, was humbled by her love.

"She has long been flying over my canvases, guiding my hand and my heart," he said of her. "I never complete a painting without asking for her 'yes' or 'no.'" He soared with her—on the ground and in the air.

Their happiness knew no bounds, and Marc's joy in his new wife gave him extra creative strength. His love for her—and for life itself—shone from all his pictures. For the rest of her life Bella would remain the major force in Marc's life and in his art.

7

"The Only Thing I Want to Do Is Make Pictures"

One day, shortly after his marriage, Marc suddenly found himself in the army, being shipped to the capital in a cattle car with other soldiers. They were brutes, he said, who shoved him out of the train and forced him to ride on the running board. Bella's brother Jacov Rosenfeld soon arranged for Marc to have a routine office job in St. Petersburg. Jacov, a brilliant young attorney and the only one of Bella's family friendly towards Marc, was director of the Office of War Economy.

In the spring of 1916 a baby girl was born to Bella and Marc. They named her Ida. During the next few tumultuous years, as they witnessed the gathering momentum of a coming revolution, Marc painted a series of pictures of Ida—in a high chair, visiting her grandparents—as well as scenes of the countryside around Vitebsk.

It was at this time that the Russian Revolution was about to take place, bringing with it great upheaval. The revolution held the promise of a new life for Jews since it promised them freedom from the Czar. To Marc Chagall, as to all the Jews of Russia, it signaled an opportunity for full citizenship and removal of the Pale. It would put an end to restrictions in the universities and to the internal passport system. Most of all, it promised an end to the slaughter of Jews. And it aroused hopes that the boldest dreams of the young generation of artists could now be realized.

When intellectuals, artists, and poets began meeting to lay the foundations of a society devoted to arts and culture, Marc attended their meetings at the Michailowsky Theatre. But when he was asked to become its director, Bella begged him to decline. His painting was all that mattered, she advised.

So they left St. Petersburg and returned once more to Vitebsk. The revolution had not really penetrated this tiny provincial city, and the war that would ultimately destroy it had not yet arrived. The Chagalls could live in relative peace. And Marc could paint again.

Settled in his in-laws' large, comfortable house with his wife and baby daughter, he completed several major works: *Double Portrait with Wine Glass*, *Promenade*, and *Above the City*. All proclaimed his love for Bella.

With his old teacher Jehuda Pen as his companion, he painted a beautiful series of the Jewish cemetery, most notably *Cemetery Gates* (1917). Poignantly expressing the tragedy of death, this was his memorial to the Jews who had been killed during the pogroms before the revolution.

His work was being exhibited frequently in St. Petersburg and in Moscow, and important collectors began to show an interest in it.

And he began writing his memoirs. He wrote in Yiddish, the language of his childhood. He was now just thirty years old, but he had been jotting down notes since 1911, when he was only twenty-four. One must wonder how he sensed then that the story of his life would some day become important.

This time of anxiety, marked by war and revolution, became one of Marc Chagall's most productive periods and saw the beginning of his rise to fame.

After the 1917 October Revolution, all previous restrictions for Jews were lifted, almost overnight. So it was not surprising that on September 12, 1918, the Minister of Culture appointed Marc Chagall Commissar of Fine Arts for Vitebsk. A short time before, Marc had submitted to him a plan to create an art school in Vitebsk. Now Marc was asked to create not only an art school, but a museum as well, teaching drawing in the schools, organizing lectures and exhibitions, and even establishing a local theater. He was about to realize his ardent desire to bring art closer to the Russian people. For the next eighteen months Marc would enjoy an experience such as has never been available to another Russian artist.

Dressed like a government official in a red Russian blouse, boots, and a cap, with a leather briefcase tucked under his arm, Marc concentrated fully on his new role. Only his long hair and pink smudges on his cheeks from his paintings betrayed the fact that he was an artist. Usually shy and anxious, he began now to feel like a man of action. He built a fine school and museum. When he went to Moscow to try to raise money for them, Bella took over as head of the academy. But even as he ran about, holding meetings late into the night, raising money, writing reports, he still found time to paint.

When he was asked to organize a festival to commemorate the first anniversary of the October Revolution he produced astonishing results. On November 6, 1918, the city of Vitebsk was transformed into a bright and joyous town. Sign painters and house painters as well as artists had been called into service, and the city was decorated with enormous red banners hanging on the buildings and spanning the streets. The most gigantic of these was by Marc himself, entitled *Man Leaping Over the City*. Triumphal arches had been built, through which thousands of participants marched, carrying flags proclaiming revolutionary slogans.

But then Marc was told how many shirts could have been made from the material used for banners, and he was asked why cows and donkeys were flying through the air in his pictures. Why hadn't the city been decorated instead with pictures of Marx and Lenin, the leaders of the Communists?

A party line was being laid down which artists were expected to follow. The Communist government mistrusted flights of imagination in art, and imposed strict rules calling for realistic "safe" art.

From this time on, things began to disintegrate around Marc. Friends and students deserted him. His school, despite its early success, began to have prob-

Bella, Marc, and Ida were hungry and cold in Moscow.

lems. Pupils took advantage of his good nature, teachers didn't want to keep up to his pace, and some began to mock him. Ingratitude seemed to be his reward for hard work.

His dreams for Vitebsk were shattered.

"It should not surprise me if my city obliterates all traces of me after some time and does not remember the person who abandoned his paintbrush, who tortured himself, suffered and tried to give art a home here, who dreamed of changing ordinary houses into museums and common citizens into artists. And then I realized that a prophet is never accepted in his own country."

In May of 1920 he took his little family and left for Moscow. But life there was bleak. By the beginning of 1918 uprisings and civil war had caused widespread famine and terrible epidemics of influenza, cholera, and typhus. People burned furniture for a little warmth. Bread was made of bran and straw. Many days there was no bread. There were freezing nights in damp beds—even the blankets were damp from the snow that came in through the roof. Often Bella would wake in the night and beg Marc, "Go and look at the baby. Is there much snow in her bed? Cover her mouth!"

But they had to stay where they were. There was no place else to go. They could no longer move back to Bella's parents' home. It had been destroyed. Some time earlier, the Rosenfelds had been terrified one evening when Russian soldiers, aware of their wealth, arrived and began to gather up precious stones, gold, silver, watches—everything of value in the three shops. Then they entered the house, thrust a revolver under Bella's mother's nose, and demanded, "The keys to the strongbox, or else . . ." They even took the silver service that had just been cleared from the dining room table. By the time they left, they had carried off everything. Bella's parents, sitting mute, their arms hanging at their sides, staring into the distance, seemed suddenly aged.

Still not satisfied, the soldiers returned a few hours later and ripped out walls and floorboards in the hope of finding hidden treasure. The crowd that had gathered in the street wept silently.

So Marc and Bella did the best they could. Every morning Marc would set out to look for a little milk for their "Idotchka." Often all he could get was a little water with starch added, which Ida refused to drink. One day, though, he came home dragging half a cow; another, a sack of flour. Despite the lack of food, Ida was growing into a beautiful child with a creamy complexion, carrot red hair, and pink cheeks like her father.

Bella, combining tenderness and the determination to survive, made it possible for her husband to continue to paint. And Marc, who had an astonishing capacity to laugh through his tears, was soon fired with enthusiasm for a new project.

Marc had long dreamed of working for the theater. Now he had been asked to paint the naked walls of the tiny Jewish Theatre in Moscow. The murals he executed here were the largest paintings he had undertaken until then, and foreshadowed the monumental works that were yet to come. One canvas alone measured more than twelve by thirty-six feet.

One of his great joys at this time was the opportunity to produce the set designs for three short plays by the great Jewish writer Sholom Aleichem. They had met at the theater and shared a vision of the world of Hasidic culture. In these designs Marc could let his imagination run free, for to him a set design became an opportunity to paint a new world. He developed a rich and original style, and he was happy again. His enthusiasm, his energy, and his natural understanding of all aspects of the theater were so contagious that he soon became the director, in charge of every aspect of the production, even the actors' make-up. In fact, his sketches for sets and costumes became a turning point in the history of the modern stage. But he was never paid for his work.

In the hope that life might be slightly less difficult and milk for Ida a little easier to obtain, Marc moved his family from Moscow to a little country village called Malachowka. But he continued to work in Moscow. Now he had to make a long, torturous train trip to Moscow every day, leaving before dawn and arriving home long after dark in the icy Russian winter. Still he found joy in the lilac blue of the early morning sky and the arches formed by the snow-covered birch trees in the deserted woods through which he walked to the train station.

Soon, in order to be able to obtain food for his family, he accepted a position as a teacher at a colony of fifty orphaned children. Now, too, he would be spared the daily train journey to Moscow. Marc, Bella, and Ida moved into the shelter and together with the children washed floors, baked bread, did kitchen chores, and pumped water from the well. Ida became friendly with some of the children and studied with them.

All the children had witnessed the brutal murders of their parents, then had roamed the streets ragged, shivering with cold and hunger, terrified, until they were taken into the shelter for children. Here they were gradually helped to return to a normal life.

Marc loved them, and they in turn learned to love him. "Comrade Chagall!" they would shout when he came in.

"They drew. They threw themselves upon colors like animals on meat," Marc recalled.

This was a difficult period in his life. He was in his early thirties and his little family was barely surviving in this freezing, famine-struck country. In 1921 "old" Zachar (he was only in his mid-fifties) was run over by an automobile and killed. Not long after, Marc's beloved brother, David, died of tuberculosis. On Marc's frail shoulders fell the financial burden of providing for his mother and sisters.

But burning with ambition, he could still manage, amid all the sadness and turmoil, to create paintings full of humor and inventiveness—an example of his indestructable spirit. These terrible years, marked by the disasters of war and revolution, were among the most productive of his life. And his fame in Moscow and St. Petersburg was growing steadily.

But he was beginning to feel hampered in his artistic freedom. Art was being influenced too much by politics, and he was an individualist: "For me, a picture has to contain elements of my conception of painting. Man is looking for something new." He felt as though he were in a straitjacket, misunderstood, an outsider in his homeland, and he was sad.

"The only thing I want to do is make pictures," he said to Bella.

He thought about his "prewar" paintings which he had left in Berlin and Paris. "Wouldn't it be sensible to build a career there?" he wondered aloud.

Encouraged by Bella, and with the help of one of his friends, Marc managed to obtain a visa. At the end of April, 1922, clad in a huge outfit of khaki canvas donated by the American Red Cross, he left for Germany. Bella, who had fractured her ankle, had to remain in Moscow with Ida. They would join him in Berlin a few months later.

Sixty-five paintings, hundreds of gouaches and drawings, and the manuscript of his memoirs, to which he had now given the title "*My Life*," and which he called "a written painting," were sent to Germany. But many of his greatest paintings had been confiscated and remained locked in Russian vaults.

The Chagalls' life in Russia had come to an end.

8

"Come Back, You're Famous"

When Marc Chagall arrived in Berlin in May, 1922, World War I had just ended and the city had become a stopping-off point between Moscow and Paris, a center of German culture. Here Marc could read newspapers (one hundred twenty were available there) and learn of the unbelievable events that had taken place in Europe while the revolution had been going on in Russia.

And he learned that he was famous. The news had not traveled to Russia. His name was known now in all the European art circles, his paintings had been exhibited, and important studies of his work had appeared in reviews.

But even with fame there was no money. All the paintings and gouaches he had left at Der Sturm Gallery were gone—sold to different collectors. The money

Herwath Walden had received for them and deposited for Chagall had been reduced to almost nothing by inflation in defeated Germany. Marc had no idea where most of his paintings were. By now they were scattered all over the world. He was able to locate and recover three: *To Russia, Asses and Others* (painted on a bedsheet and portraying the entire world of his childhood—the *isbas,* domes, and steeples of Vitebsk); *The Poet;* and *I and My Village.*

While in Germany, something happened that would set Marc on another, and extremely important, course in his art. An art dealer and editor asked Marc to produce a series of etchings to illustrate *My Life* for publication in German.

In order to learn this technique, Marc took lessons from Hermann Struck, one of the greatest graphic artists in Europe. Marc immediately became wildly enthusiastic about this exciting new craft. Within three weeks Marc had prepared fifteen plates for his memoirs, then added five more.

He was fascinated by all the new possibilities. He created not just etchings, but experimented briefly with woodcuts and lithographs as well. From the outset Marc showed a total mastery of the medium and produced a series of illustrations that captured completely the poetic quality of his paintings and gouaches.

For the next sixteen months he worked hard on *My Life* and other challenging projects. With his love for Bella and Ida, who had joined him, and a few old friends who had come to Berlin, life was even happier and more fulfilling.

The text of *My Life* was never published in German,

for no one could capture in translation Marc's poetic Yiddish writing. It would remain for Bella to translate it into French years later. But the etchings were published separately under the title *Mein Leben*.

Soon after he arrived in Berlin, Marc received a letter from his old friend in Paris, Blaise Cendrars. "Come back, you're famous, and Vollard is waiting for you," it said. Ambroise Vollard, whose celebrated gallery in Paris was filled with works by Cézanne, Renoir, Bonnard, Pissaro, Van Gogh, Picasso, Matisse, and others, had discovered Chagall through Cendrars *after* Marc had left Paris.

Marc and Bella were overjoyed. Marc had always hoped for a chance to return. It had sustained him through all the dark days in Russia. Now they made hurried plans to leave Berlin. They managed to obtain the necessary papers to allow them to cross the French border, and on one of those glorious days that mark the end of summer, Marc, Bella, and Ida arrived in Paris. It was September 1, 1923.

After the horror and terror of the revolution in Russia, Paris once again appeared to Marc as a haven. Joyous, exultant, he felt as though he had come home. A new phase in his colorful life was about to begin. Years later, remembering the moment when he first felt the pavement stones of Paris under his feet, he confided to a friend, "I returned to France because I felt this country was my real homeland."

This time he knew Paris—its geography, its people—and he had friends waiting for him there. He was no longer the frightened young boy from Vitebsk.

With his wife and child at his side, he was an artist in full possession of his art, confident of where he was headed. The next eighteen years would be the happiest he was to know.

As soon as Marc had Bella and Ida settled in an apartment, he went to La Ruche to retrieve the paintings he had left there nine years before. As he pushed open the heavy iron gate and entered the courtyard, then climbed the worn staircase to his studio, he was overwhelmed by memories of his youth. But his heart sank when he discovered that the wire he had twisted around the lock was gone and the lock had been replaced.

When he knocked at the door it was opened by a stranger who explained that this was his studio. All Marc's possessions were gone. No, said the stranger, he didn't know where they were.

Marc was stunned. More than one hundred fifty paintings had vanished. This staggering loss, added to the loss of 40 oils and 160 other pictures in Berlin, deprived him of most of his early work.

Since many people in Paris believed that Marc Chagall had died during the Russian Revolution, some of his paintings had been given away, some had been sold, and some had even been used by the new caretaker at La Ruche as a roof for her rabbit hutch. Frustrated, angry, heartbroken, Marc tried to reconstruct from memory or photos some of the lost work.

And he went to see Vollard. Ambroise Vollard had a passion for beautiful books, and his genius lay in commissioning prominent artists to illustrate important texts. As a result, he helped to develop a new art form: the illustrated book.

Now Vollard asked Chagall to illustrate a book. Excited at the prospect of using his newly learned craft of etching once again, Marc chose *Dead Souls* by Gogol, an exiled Russian writer with whom he identified. He completed 117 plates in two years. His illustrations were a reflection of his deepest feelings and movingly portrayed Russian life and the Russian world he remembered. He found poetry in the everyday life of ordinary people.

When the plates for *Dead Souls* were completed, Vollard asked Chagall to illustrate the *Fables* of La Fontaine, a French classic read by all French schoolchildren. Bella patiently translated the stories word for word from the French into Russian for him. He managed to capture the *essence,* or feeling of the stories, and between 1928 and 1931 he executed one hundred plates. His illustrations are extraordinary in the richness and variety of his imagination and technique.

By now, Marc had moved far away from the world of the Montparnasse and La Ruche of 1910 to 1914. He had a wife and child, a reputation across Europe and a reassuring financial position based on Vollard's commissions and steady sales. He had never known such success. Many people in Paris were buying pictures in those days—and particularly prints, which were cheaper than paintings. This was the period between the two world wars, before the stock market crash of 1929 and before the beginning of Nazism.

Soon after their return to Paris in 1923, Bella persuaded Marc to travel. From then on they became incapable of remaining in one place. This need to travel, this restlessness, remained with him for the rest of his life.

From 1924 until 1931 they wandered around the

French provinces. Marc seemed to prefer the remote villages and farms of France, perhaps because of a need to feel close to the earth—to the animal world with its roosters, goats, cows, and oxen, which had cast their spell over his childhood and become the "stuff" of his dreams. Wherever they went he always carried a small sketchbook in which he scribbled.

In 1926, vacationing near Toulon, he was struck by the magical coloring of the area in the south of France known as the Midi. On his first visit to Nice, on the Riviera, he was overwhelmed by the brightness of the Mediterranean Sea, and thrilled by the bunches of flowers Bella brought home from the old Ponchettes flower market day after day. He seemed to carry these images with him ever after. From then on, there were more and more flowers in his painting. They became for him the essence of love, gaiety, and beauty.

In the late 1920s Marc realized that he would probably never return to Russia, and he missed it deeply. So from time to time he visited Switzerland, where the snow-covered mountains and majestic fir trees reminded him of his lost homeland.

And through it all, he and Bella were described as a happy pair of lovers. She was an ideal companion for Marc, and he was almost incapable of action without her. She created a lively, loving atmosphere at home that allowed him to develop his art. Her influence on his work was enormous. He considered no painting completed until she had approved. She never actually told him what to do, but she knew, instinctively, the weak point of any composition. Sometimes he didn't agree with her opinion. Then, furious, he would turn the painting towards the wall. Later, when his rage had subsided, he would turn it back and change it in line with her suggestion. Although he painted many subjects, some of his most important works of this period are portraits of Bella.

Marc's paintings were being shown in galleries in London and Paris, and in 1926, he had his first exhibition in New York under the auspices of Pierre Matisse, art dealer and son of the painter Henri Matisse.

In 1927 the Chagalls left their apartment in Paris and moved to a small house with a garden in Boulogne. But before they moved they gave a birthday party for Ida, who was now eight years old. Many old friends attended.

Marc loved to entertain his friends. He was an actor who had the perfect timing of a comedian. He would put on a mustache and improvise skits in the garden. He was full of invention, and there was much laughter.

In Boulogne he painted a steady stream of happy pictures filled with rich, lavish colors—pictures that proclaimed his love for Bella, for Ida, for France, for flowers, for the art of painting. It was one of the happiest times of his life.

His success knew no bounds. He could hardly keep up with the commissions that were pouring in. Articles on his art were appearing in newspapers in Paris and in Germany, special issues of art magazines were devoted to him, and his place in the art world was secure. He was considered one of the leaders of the School of Paris, and he exhibited in many shows as a French artist. One reviewer, comparing him to Pablo Picasso, said, "Picasso is the triumph of intelligence, Chagall the glory of the heart."

Soon Vollard had a new plan. He wanted Chagall to do a series of lithographs on the circus. As a child in Russia Marc had occasionally gone to the circus with his brother and sisters, and he had probably seen traveling acrobats as they went from city to city. He never forgot them.

In France, every Thursday was a school holiday, so he began to take Ida to the circus once a week. He was as childishly delighted by it as his little daughter. Often, he also attended with Vollard, who had season tickets. Sometimes he went three times in one week. He was fascinated by the unreal and mysterious aspect of the spectacle, its electric quality of tension, the charm of the bareback riders, and the grace of the acrobats and the flying trapeze artists. And he loved the clowns.

"Who isn't a clown, complete with funny hat? . . . people are a circus themselves," he said. The circus was casting a spell on him. It began to take an important place in his painting.

In 1930, at the age of forty-three, Chagall was described by the writer André Salmon as "clean-shaven,

Marc took Ida to the circus once a week.

and curly-haired as a lamb, eyes like heavenly wild flowers, a dancer's step, the dance before the vaulting circus ladder." The frail adolescent who resembled a thin tightrope walker had become a solid robust man, yet one still full of dynamism.

It was at this time, while Chagall was still working on the *Fables*, that Vollard had the genius to propose to him that he do a series of illustrations for the Bible. Chagall was overjoyed with the idea. Now, finally, he would be able to immerse himself in the images that had long haunted his imagination.

As he began to think about this enormous new undertaking, his Hasidic upbringing came more and more into his thinking. The Hasids' unfaltering faith in God, their hope in the face of despair, their love of music, and their love for stories and storytelling would all find their way into his etchings.

He began to think about visiting Palestine. He knew he didn't need a trip to the Holy Land to "document" his illustrations, but he felt intuitively that such a trip would enhance the images already bubbling in his mind.

"I wasn't seeing the Bible, I was dreaming it," he explained.

So in February, 1931, with Bella and Ida, he journeyed to Palestine. There, as they traveled the winding roads of Judea, climbing towards Jerusalem, he was stirred with emotion. He felt a part of this land of kings and prophets.

As biblical themes from his childhood came back to him, he began to paint outdoors, where the light of Palestine sang in his heart like no other light had before. He completed a series of gouaches filled with lyricism and drama that would serve as the basis for his etchings.

"I love the Bible," he said, "and I love the people who created it. Do you know what I would do if I were free? I wouldn't do any more paintings to be sold . . . I would spend the rest of my life painting scenes from the Bible the way I have always seen them."

And he saw them in his own way. While his etchings related to the biblical texts, he managed to enliven them with unusual or unexpected compositions and abrupt shifts. Here again Hasidic tradition could be felt. Hasidic stories were frequently disconnected: they had holes, gaps, sudden transitions, and omitted explanations. Sholem Aleichem's stories were often like this. Now Marc Chagall's were also. His pictures showed no concern for the usual rules of composition. His paintings were the dreams that he dreamed with his eyes open. Perhaps he believed as did the Hasidic Rabbi Nahman of Bratislava who said, "Most people believe that stories are made to put you to sleep; me, I tell them to wake people up."

Marc Chagall's pictures did, indeed, wake people up. In them, he showed us the patriarchs, kings, and prophets of the Bible in all their weaknesses and strengths. When he painted his memory of an unmistakably Jewish mourner in Vitebsk to portray Abraham's profound grief at the death of Sarah (*Abraham Weeping for Sarah*), Abraham's sadness became everyone's sadness. His prophets were simply the people of his small Jewish town clad in cap and caftan.

Although he was painting in the vivid light of Pal-

71

estine, most of his illustrations for *The Bible* use darker Russian landscapes as background. In Chagall's mind the Bible, Vitebsk, and Russia were all the same: they were the lands of his faith and dreams. Perhaps it is this that gives his paintings their unique power.

In Palestine and Safed he painted indoors as well, hoping to preserve something of the spiritual world he already sensed would be threatened. But his *Synagogue at Safed*, now in the Stedelijk Museum in Amsterdam, is bathed in sunlight, heralding his later use of stained glass to express his religious belief that light and color come from within.

In April, as the family prepared to return home to France, Chagall reflected on his stay in Palestine. He had been moved by the Holy Land, yet he had no desire to live there. But he sensed in his silent Bella a deep tug to stay.

On his return to Paris, Chagall, in a burst of inspiration, set to work on the etchings for *The Bible*. From 1931 until Vollard's accidental death in 1939, Chagall completed sixty-six plates. The entire work, 105 plates, was an enormous task that would take him twenty-five years to finish. Often, Ida, now fifteen, helped him select the biblical passages for each etching. *The Bible* would prove to be his masterpiece in the field of graphic art. In fact, it has been called the single greatest masterpiece of engraving of our age. His etchings are marvels of patient craftsmanship, but his style seems natural.

"It seems to me that I would have lacked something if, aside from color, I had not also busied myself at a moment of my life with engraving and lithographs. From my earliest youth, when I first began to use a pencil, I searched for that something that could spread out like a great river pouring from the distant, beckoning shores. When I held a lithographic stone or copper plate, it seemed to me that I could put all my sorrows and joys into them," he said years later.

Vollard, though, was not interested in publishing any of Chagall's illustrations. He paid Chagall for them, but he stored them in his cellar, like fine wine. Like a miser, he wanted only to possess them.

"He never even glanced at my work when I delivered the last copper plate," Chagall sadly recalled years later. "When he died, they found all my plates stacked in his basement, covered with dust."

Dead Souls was finally published in 1948 and the *Fables* three years later. *The Bible* was published in 1956. All were done by Pierre Tériade who took over Vollard's business after his death.

9

The Wandering Jew

By the 1930s the Chagalls were financially secure, and they began to travel regularly. When they visited Holland in 1932 and saw Rembrandt's engravings of biblical subjects, they were profoundly moved by them, and Marc's attachment to Rembrandt intensified. In 1934 they went to Spain, where he was impressed by the paintings of Goya and El Greco. A year later, traveling in Vilna and Warsaw, Poland, they were disturbed by the isolation of the Jews and by visible signs of anti-Semitism. Adolph Hitler had come to power in Germany in 1933, and it was then that the systematic persecution of the Jews had begun.

During this time, in 1934, Marc's beloved daughter, Ida, eighteen years old, radiant, blue-eyed, and charming, married Michel Gorday, a young lawyer also of Russian Jewish descent not much older than she. The two had been childhood friends. Marc celebrated the marriage in a painting that is considered one of the highest achievements of his career, *The Bride's Armchair.*

But now, as the Nazis goose-stepped steadily toward another world war, and the rising tragedy of the Jews became increasingly apparent, Marc's pictures began to change. His floating lovers, his flowers, his joyous colors were replaced by *isbas* in flames. His colors became harsher, his lines stiffer. He painted Vitebsk as a symbol of suffering Russia.

He was experiencing the troubling concerns of both artist and Jew. The Nazi regime ordered his works removed from German museums. Many were destroyed. Some were slashed and burned in public.

He was also having difficulty obtaining the French citizenship for which he had applied because of his earlier role as Commissar of Fine Arts in Vitebsk. He finally became a French citizen in 1937. It had taken four years.

It was at this time that Chagall became close to Picasso, whose own country, Spain's, torment echoed Chagall's. From 1936 to 1939 the two men often met to

discuss politics. They never discussed art; their opin-
ions were too different there. But as they sat in a cafe in
Montparnasse and mourned the fate of their respective
homelands, they doodled on matchboxes to keep their
fingers busy. Then, each time they parted, they exchanged these "works of art." Ultimately, Ida had an
entire collection of matchboxes decorated by Picasso.

Deeply stricken by the sorrow of what was happen-
ing, Marc Chagall took refuge in his imagination. Painting, the language he knew best, became his answer to
war and massacre.

Now, as Picasso painted his huge masterpiece *Guernica* in response to the German terror bombing of the
Basque town of Guernica on April 26, 1937, Chagall
painted *White Crucifixion*, his own cry of anguish over
the Nazi persecution of the Jews.

White Crucifixion was probably directly inspired by
specific events: the *Aktion* of June 15, 1938, when 1,500
Jews were taken to concentration camps; the synagogues that were set on fire in Munich and Nuremberg;
and the pogroms there the same year.

Chagall, as did other Jewish artists of the twentieth
century, adopted the Crucifixion, or death of Christ, as
a poignant reminder of the suffering of Jews. For him
Christ became a powerful symbol of a man alone, whose
heart was filled with love even as he was the victim of
all the evil in the world. Chagall's Christ was clearly a
Jew, a symbol of the martyred Jewish people. The
Hebrew inscription in *White Crucifixion*, "Jesus of
Nazareth, King of the Jews," the loincloth covering
Christ cut from a Jewish prayer shawl, and the seven-
branched menorah at his feet all serve to prove this. The

scenes that frame the cross—a synagogue in flames, a Jew running to rescue a burning Torah scroll, storm troopers destroying the *isbas*, refugees trapped under the extended arms of the cross, while in the heavens the prophets grieve—emphasize the Jewishness of this Christ. Chagall's Christ is not a savior. He is the universal Jew who suffers, but remains indestructible.

On September 1, 1939, when the Germans invaded Poland and World War II was officially declared, Marc Chagall was at the peak of his career. He had just been awarded the coveted Carnegie Prize, and he had had an exhibition of his work in 1933, in Basel, Switzerland, which gave him recognition as one of the great artists of the twentieth century and placed him on equal footing with Picasso and Matisse. At the age of fifty-three he was healthy, productive, affluent—a celebrated artist and a prominent French citizen.

But now he was forced to leave Paris and to move his pictures as well. Some of his paintings were smuggled out of the country, across the border to Spain by a relative who was willing to risk his life. Many of his paintings were taken by Germans who ransacked his studio, and they were never to be found again. Once again Chagall was depleted by war.

In the spring of 1940, just as the Nazis were marching on Paris, the Chagalls moved to Gordes, a beautiful, stony village near Avignon, in the south of France. This area had not yet been occupied by the Germans. They loved the unspoiled beauty of the countryside, its trees bent by the strong winds of the *mistral*. In this lovely setting Marc began to paint with brilliant colors once again. When the peasants who lived in the area brought him baskets of grapes and figs, he painted still lifes of them that are filled with a zest for life. Perhaps they were his final farewell to his years of happiness between the two world wars.

He seemed totally unconscious of the danger he was in. Soon Varian Fry, director of the Emergency Rescue Committee, and Harry Bingham, American vice-consul in Marseille, came to see him. Their arrival in the tiny village in a big American car caused a sensation. When the men relayed an invitation from the Museum of Modern Art in New York to come to the United States, Chagall asked playfully, "But are there trees and cows in America?" He refused their offer of help. Then he added, "The Germans wouldn't dare bother me."

He was wrong. Marc and Bella were arrested by the police who generally handed over Jews to the Gestapo. But Harry Bingham intervened, and the terrified pair were released.

Marc and Bella decided to leave France immediately. On May 7, the date for which they had waited because Marc considered seven his lucky number (he had been born on the seventh day of the seventh month in 1887), they followed a secret escape route and, with forged passports provided by the Emergency Rescue Committee, crossed the Spanish border at Canfranc, then went on to Madrid. Here Bella, seized by a tragic premonition, solemnly announced that she would never see France again. And Marc, saddened at bidding farewell to France—and to his past—and knowing full well that he was leaving behind precious family whom he might never see again, wrote a poem that begins:

A wall rises up between me and mine,
A mountain covered with graves and grass.

Their luggage—eight hundred pounds of packing
cases and trunks containing five hundred paintings and
hundreds of gouaches and drawings, Marc's entire out-
put of the last few years—was impounded by customs
in one last attempt by the Gestapo to get hold of his
work. It was many months before Ida, who had stayed
behind with her husband, managed to have the paintings released. Resourceful and determined, they then
accompanied the paintings to America on a forty-three
day crossing of the Atlantic Ocean. This was just one of
many instances throughout their lives where Ida's fierce
devotion to her father was apparent.

On May 11 Marc and Bella arrived in Lisbon, from
where they sailed for New York. Once again, Marc Chagall became the wandering Jew.

10

"Where Shall I Shed My Tears?"

On June 23, 1941, just as the Nazis were marching into Russia, Marc and Bella arrived in New York. Art dealer Pierre Matisse, son of the artist Henri Matisse, met them at the pier and took them to the Hotel St. Moritz, where he had rented a room for them overlooking Central Park. Matisse was already Marc's American dealer, and the two would continue a friendly relationship for the rest of Marc's life.

Soon Marc became a familiar if somewhat bizarre figure as he strolled in the neighborhood in his Montparnasse attire of velvet jacket, checked shirt, and no tie. He loved to walk, often walking for miles exploring Jewish neighborhoods in Manhattan, imagining himself back in the Vitebsk of his childhood. But he never felt comfortable in this big city. And he never learned to speak much English—or to love America. Nothing could dull the pain of leaving France.

By now the Holocaust was at its peak. Before it ended six million Jews would be massacred in German concentration camps.

Struggling to understand the English language, Marc listened with anguish to news broadcasts of the German offensive in Russia, and along with it the burning of Vitebsk. His love for his native land was reawakened, and his deep-rooted Russian Jewishness intensified.

He began to paint a series of paintings of "Jewish" crucifixions reminiscent of his *White Crucifixion* of 1939. Work became Marc's greatest comfort during the six years that he remained in New York.

More and more artists began to arrive in New York: Max Ernst, André Breton, Jacques Lipchitz, Piet Mondrian, Chaim Gross. Soon all were represented in a show, "Artists in Exile," mounted by Pierre Matisse.

Chagall was, indeed, almost literally an artist in exile. He was restless and uneasy, unable to adjust to the rhythms of New York City, finding its vastness cold and forbidding. Despite his reputation in France, he was not well known in America. Although Matisse showed his work, and some of his art sold, for the most part he was ignored.

But even in these trying times his essentially joyous nature bubbled forth. He never lost the capacity to be a clown and to laugh at himself. He charmed all who met him. And his beautiful Bella, often reserved yet full of high spirits, too, always had a huge tray filled with sweets and good things to eat ready for guests who came to visit.

By then they had moved to a tiny apartment at 4 East 74 Street, which Bella furnished to resemble their Paris studio. She managed to give it an atmosphere of European hospitality that was much appreciated by their friends. These included the philosopher Jacques Maritain and his wife Raissa, the critic Lionello Venturi, the Yiddish writer Joseph Opatoshu, and the distinguished art historian Meyer Schapiro. Marc also became friendly with the artist Chaim Gross. The two men dropped into each other's studios frequently and spoke Yiddish together. When Marc and Bella moved to Connecticut to escape the summer heat of the city, they met American sculptor Alexander Calder, who became another good friend.

In the spring of 1942 an opportunity presented itself to Marc that steered his fantasy in a new direction—away from the horrors of war. Ballet Theatre commissioned him to design the scenery and costumes for the ballet *Aleko,* based on a poem called "The Gypsies" by the Russian poet Pushkin, and set to the music of *Piano Trio* by Tchaikovsky. Soon Marc and Léonide Massine, the choreographer, were happily at work together.

Every day for several months Massine arrived at Marc's apartment, where the two men worked closely together, all the while listening to the music of Tchaikovsky on the record player. For Marc and Bella these months working with Massine were among the happiest of their stay in America. Years later, just a few bars of the *Piano Trio* were enough to evoke wonderful memories.

Because of technical reasons the first performance of *Aleko* was given in Mexico City, rather than New York. Early in August they all traveled to Mexico. There Marc painted the four large backdrops while Bella supervised the making of the costumes in a variety of colored materials, many of which had to be hand painted.

Marc worked day and night on every detail. He was painting the scenery and touching up the costumes to get the colors exactly as he wanted almost as the curtain was rising on opening night.

The premiere, on September 8, 1942, was a triumph. Dance and scenery, sets and costumes, color and movement had blended to produce a "Chagallesque" whole dedicated to music. The cheering audience called again and again for Marc Chagall. He took nineteen curtain calls. His creative imagination had reached new heights.

The New York opening at the Metropolitan Opera House less than a month later was equally a triumph. John Martin, dance critic of *The New York Times*, wrote of the backdrops: "So exciting are they in their own right that more than once one wishes all those people would quit getting in front of them."

The beauty of the Mexican landscape and the intense light of the tropics had inspired in Marc a new color sensibility, and his work after his return to New York showed a deep sympathy with Mexico and the Mexican people.

It was just two years later, in September of 1944, while Marc and Bella were on holiday in Cranberry Lake in the Adirondak Mountains in upstate New York, that tragedy struck. A few days earlier, on August 25, they had listened spellbound to the news of the liberation of Paris. Sitting with their ears pressed to the radio, their hearts beating with the sound of the tolling bells of Notre Dame in the background, they tried hard to understand the English words of the broadcaster.

Bella wanted to return to France immediately. She longed to see her beloved second homeland. Excitedly, they made plans to leave on September 3 or 4. But her dream was not to be fulfilled.

Bella had just finished writing her memoirs, begun on their return from Poland in 1939, where she had been shocked by the rising tide of anti-Semitism. She had felt a need then to document and preserve her memories of the warm family circle in which she had celebrated the Jewish holidays, and of her first meeting with Marc.

She wrote movingly and poetically in Yiddish, the language of her childhood, which she had not used since their marriage. As she wrote, Bella, who had for so many years devoted her life to her husband, finally discovered her own creative talent in her writing, and was able to reclaim the vanished world of her childhood. Until now her creativity had been channeled into Marc's work. She was his supreme critic. In *Ma Vie* he had written, "May our deceased parents bless *our* painting."

Now Marc came upon her one day ("fresh and beautiful as always," he described her) carefully arranging her notes. When he asked her, "Why this sudden tidiness?" she answered with a wan smile, "So you'll know where everything is."

Then suddenly, the young and beautiful Bella complained that her throat was burning. Marc kept making hot tea for her. The next day she was so feverish that he took her to the local hospital, a Catholic institution. But several days before, in another place nearby where they had been staying, Bella had seen a sign indicating that Jews were not welcome. An exception had obviously been made for the famous artist Marc Chagall and his wife.

Now, when Bella saw the nuns at the hospital and was asked to indicate her religion on the admission form, in her high fever and highly emotional state, she refused and begged Marc to take her home. By the next day, when Marc did have her admitted to the hospital, it was too late to save her. She had a streptococcus infection. In those days the only drug that could check it was penicillin. The drug was new and reserved for military use and, therefore, not available.

Bella's last words to Marc were, "My notebooks . . ." There was a sudden, loud clap of thunder and with it a violent rainstorm at six o'clock on the evening of September 2, 1944, and Bella was gone.

"Everything went dark," Chagall wrote.

Ida arrived just in time to witness her mother's death.

Bella had been Marc's muse, his guardian angel. She had been a brilliant intellectual, a quietly refined woman whose personality melted into his completely and on whom he relied entirely. He called her his *nishoma*, his soul. She had given meaning to his life and inspiration to his art. She had been the center of his universe, and he had loved her passionately.

Her love had been an inexhaustible source of romantic wonder for him, and her radiant image—as fiancée, wife, mother—in whole series of portraits, drawings, and compositions recounts their remarkable relationship. The simple marble tombstone he carved for her is eloquent testament to their love.

Now his hair began to turn white almost overnight. For nine months he was unable to paint. The pictures in his studio were turned to the wall. He found comfort, with Ida, in translating Bella's memoirs from Yiddish into French, executing thirty-six sensitive pen and ink drawings to illustrate them. They would be published in Switzerland after the war under the title, *Lumières Allumées* (*Burning Lights*). "Her words and phrases were a wash of color over a canvas," Marc said of them. And he expressed his grief in his own poem:

> *My love*
>
> Where is my love
> Where is my dream
> Where is the joy of my lifetime
> Which lasts to the setting of the sun

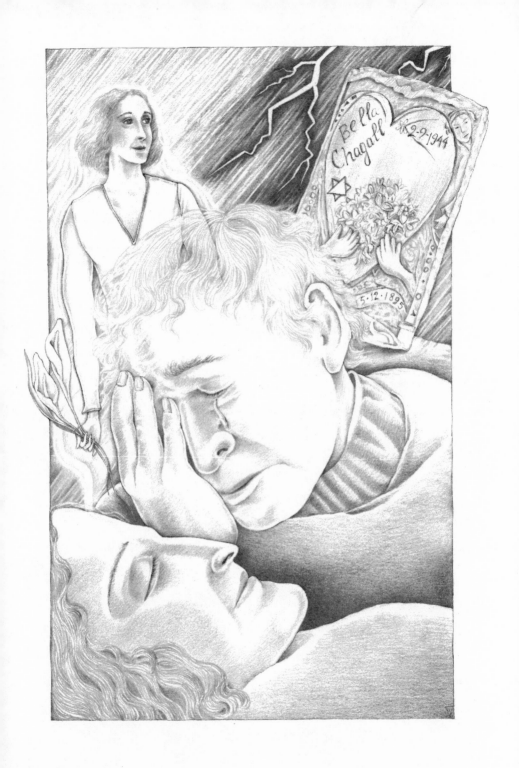

"He had loved her passionately."

MARC CHAGALL

I see you at every step
I see you in my sleep
I see you in my sadness
I see you in loneliness

Day and night I hear you
The world I live in is closed

The light is fading
Night is coming
Where should I hide my colors
Where shall I shed my tears

11

A New Beginning

Back in New York, Alexander Calder, shattered by Bella's death, became a support to Marc in his grief. He would often drop into Marc's studio to keep him company. One day he brought him a small, gay, brightly colored mobile with a man's body and the head of a goat to cheer him.

At the beginning of the winter Marc moved, with Ida and her husband, to a new double apartment at 75 Riverside Drive, with spectacular views of the Hudson River. Here Marc had a vast studio and bedroom, allowing him complete privacy and independence. By the spring, he was painting again. But the desire to return to France had faded. It wouldn't be the same without his Bella. And, he later confided, he was "afraid to rub shoulders with people who had sent Jews to gas chambers."

"It was the first time in my life I ever stopped painting," he said later. "If the work didn't go on it would kill me. A day without work is never a real day for me. I have to feel I've taken a step forward, solved a problem, made some discovery."

Now, with the music of Mozart, his favorite composer, playing in the background, Marc cut the large picture *Circus People* in two and painted over the left-hand side, transforming it into a new picture entitled *Around Her*, a poignant memorial to Bella. Later the right side became *The Wedding Candles*, its title referring to Bella's book.

Marc often cut up pictures on which he had been working for a long time, but which didn't satisfy him. He never actually discarded them. Instead, he would transform them. Sometimes he even turned them upside down and they became completely new pictures. But he was careful to sign them before he put them away so he would remember which was right side up. He looked on them as his children and could not accept their failure.

The miracle of painting served to reawaken in him his latent love of life. Once again his wonderful smile broke through, and friends began to see the Marc Chagall they remembered. The pain of loss was being eased by work.

"Painting was as necessary to me as bread. It seemed like a window I could escape out of, to take flight to another world," he said years later.

At Ida's request, a tall, slender, attractive young Englishwoman named Virginia Haggard, a friend of a friend of Ida's, began to come regularly to mend Marc's socks and to pose, with her five-year-old daughter Jean, for Ida, who was trying to paint. When Ida's housekeeper suddenly quit, Ida asked the young woman if she would come to the apartment every day to look after her father and to prepare his meals.

"She took me into the big studio overlooking the Hudson River and he came forward smiling. His shyness was the same as mine," Virginia described their first meeting.

Virginia was the daughter of a British diplomat and had been born in Paris, studied art there, and spoke fluent French. Her own marriage of ten years had fallen apart, and she was struggling to support herself and her daughter.

Slowly, quietly, gently, these two lonely people were able to breathe life back into one another. With Bella's beautiful dark eyes looking down on them from a girlhood photo, Marc and Virginia talked to each other of their childhoods, of their families, of their hopes. Soon they began to love each other.

One day Marc was asked by the New York City Ballet to design the sets and costumes for Igor Stravinsky's *Firebird*, with choreography by George Balanchine. A legend of triumphant love, the ballet is based on an old Russian fairy tale about a princess held captive by a wicked magician, then set free by a prince with the help of the marvelous Firebird.

To escape the heat of the city, Ida rented a huge, sprawling summer house in Sag Harbor, on Long Island, with ample room for her father to work. Virginia and Jean were invited to accompany them. It was here that Marc, jotting down vague ideas, sketching feverishly in pencil, then soaking the sketches in pools of color, could let his imagination run free, and he achieved breathtaking results. Working with Stravinsky's explosive music always in the background, he painted an enormous curtain and three backdrops and drew the designs for eighty costumes.

The opening curtain, a bird-woman with outstretched wings soaring across a midnight blue sky, reflects Marc's newfound love. Through Virginia, Marc had become the very Firebird he was portraying. A new period in his life was beginning.

Marc, embarrassed by his relationship with Virginia (they had not married), but very much in love with her, bought a simple wooden house in High Falls, a rural section of the Catskill Mountains. He, Virginia, and Jean went to live there. Marc began work on illustrations (color lithographs) for *One Thousand and One Nights*, making rapid sketches that he spread all over the living room floor to dry while Virginia read the stories aloud to him, as Bella had done so many years before. Marc loved to be read to as he worked. He worked quickly, carried away by ideas that flashed into his mind, and unconcerned with any obstacles that appeared. "Art is a deluge," he explained to Virginia, "but a controlled deluge."

In April Marc was honored by a splendid exhibition of his paintings at the Museum of Modern Art in New York. Included were a number of his early works, which had been sent over from Europe. His joy at seeing these again was boundless. Virginia has compared it to that of a father retrieving his lost children. He told her then that his favorite painting was *The Praying Jew,* and that for years in Russia he had kept it under his bed to protect it.

In May Marc finally made the long-dreamed-of trip back to France. Ida had gone ahead to arrange an exhibition of her father's paintings at the Musée d'Art Moderne in Paris. Ida was now pouring all her tremendous energy and bubbling enthusiasm into promoting her father's work. Virginia remained in High Falls. She was awaiting the birth of their child.

David, named for Marc's brother, was born in New York on June 22, 1946, and Marc and Virginia exchanged joyous telegrams. But Marc didn't return until August.

In accordance with Marc's wishes, David was circumcised, and Virginia attempted to bring him up as a Jew. She herself was not Jewish and had resisted Marc's suggestions that she adopt the Jewish religion. Despite the fact that during his early years in St. Petersburg and in Paris he had become an "assimilated" Jew and had given up formal observance of Jewish ritual, Marc's Jewish heritage was at all times an integral part of his life. He was caught midway between the culture of his childhood, which shaped his personality, and the culture of St. Petersburg and Paris, which shaped his way of life. He had left his past behind, yet he carried it with him. His Judaism was important to him, and the difference between his background and Virginia's troubled him. He once wrote, "Were I not a Jew, with all the significance I put into that word, I would not be an artist at all."

Now he began to compare Virginia more and more to Bella. He was still filled with conflict and guilt over the presence of one and the memory of the other, and his pictures of this period were of both of them.

In that same year Marc completed *The Falling Angel,* his first successful attempt at large easel painting. Begun in 1923 and worked on again in 1933, it had taken him twenty-four years to complete. It was his interpretation of the nightmarish events that had provoked World War II.

"That picture changed everything," he said of it years later. "I started to realize that studio paintings weren't everything, that, in fact, I had to get out of the studio . . . to really work in depth."

Overall, Marc was joyously happy with Virginia and the children, he loved the seclusion of their house in the countryside, and he settled down to a happy and fruitful period. He even sent a photo of himself with David to Picasso in France. Picasso, touched by this gesture, hung the photo on a wall in his bedroom.

In spite of Ida's constant urging from Paris for him to

return, Marc was content to remain in America. "I'm a foreigner here and at the same time I'm at home because I'm a Jew," he said. New York was full of Russian Jews who shared his exile. And the few months he had just spent in France had reawakened his alarm at the deep roots of anti-Semitism there. Perhaps, also, he recognized that once back in France his celebrity would intrude on the intimate family life he and Virginia had established, and their joyous "honeymoon" would come to an end.

But Ida persisted. "Paris is waiting for you, and so are we," she wrote. Letters, phone calls, telegrams all insisted that Marc belonged in France. Finally, in August, 1948, Marc, Virginia, Jean, and David sailed for France together. This was the first public acknowledgment that Marc made of his new family.

They settled in Orgeval, near Paris, and Marc happily reestablished contact with old friends in the literary and art world. There were many exhibitions of his work throughout Europe, and he was awarded first prize for graphic art at the Venice Biennale. They visited Italy, where Marc was overwhelmed by the paintings of Titian and Tintoretto.

In 1950, lured by the intense sun and flowers of the south of France, they moved to Vence, an ancient walled town in the hills above Cannes. Here Marc's studio windows afforded a view of the brilliant blue of the Mediterranean Sea. Their villa, called Les Collines (The Hills), was surrounded by palm trees and orange groves. Virginia immediately set about having the dilapidated house transformed into a cheerful white one with green shutters and a roof of curved tiles.

Now, for the first time since the war, all Marc's belongings were under the same roof. The furniture that had been left behind when he and Bella escaped from France and all his paintings were finally assembled here. Virginia undertook the huge task of having all the watercolors, drawings, and sketches—hundreds of them—mounted and put away in specially made large portfolios. She photographed every picture and filed the photos in albums with numbers and titles. She took great pleasure in helping Marc, and in feeling needed. She handled all his correspondence, and she often squared off his pictures and drew in the rough lines with charcoal, a mechanical process he didn't enjoy.

But it was Ida (divorced the year before from Michel Gorday) who handled all the business arrangements. She was her father's confidante and ally, and she worked hard to promote his fame until the powerful art dealer Aimé Maeght came into the picture and won the exclusive right to represent him. Maeght had a natural flair for recognizing true quality in art, as well as a brilliant business mind. Ultimately he would establish the Maeght Foundation, an important institution dedicated to the art of the twentieth century, in the neighboring town of St. Paul de Vence.

In Vence Marc set to work in earnest. He was inspired once again by the exquisite light he had missed in America and by the glory of the flowers in the area. His work began to grow in scope and brilliance. Picasso was convinced that no one since Renoir had the feeling for light that Chagall did. Marc painted bouquets of flowers from the Ponchettes Flower Market in Nice, he painted fruits and vegetables in Provençal ceramic bowls, and, if they would sit still long enough, he painted pictures of Jean and David.

Marc had a deep need for music while he worked, and Virginia found herself winding up the record player continuously. Sometimes, if the work were going well, he would sing in a warm, melodious voice.

Perhaps this area in which he was living was the inspiration, too, for a new field of endeavor, for now he tried his hand at pottery making. At first he simply painted ready-made ceramic pieces. Later, he modelled the figures in the clay from his own imaginative world. Ultimately he would also try his hand at sculpture in stone.

For a short time he worked at a potter's studio with Picasso and Matisse. But when Picasso and Matisse quickly threw and baked their pottery, then went to see how Marc was doing, he was embarrassed. He could not work in front of people, and created nothing until his friends left. Creation for Marc Chagall was a mystery, a miracle, not a craft.

Later, when Matisse was ill and bedridden, Marc and Virginia would often visit him in his lovely old house in Cimiez, high above Nice, overlooking the bay. There the elderly painter would lie in bed and draw on the ceiling with a stick of charcoal attached to the end of a bamboo pole, or cut out large pieces of brilliantly colored paper which his secretary would then paste onto a board. Matisse was the only painter whose studio Marc ever visited. He was proud of the fact that Ida had posed for Matisse, although he was jealous of her admiration for him.

Marc was always wary of Picasso, but he liked

Matisse, and often walked to the exquisite little chapel Matisse had decorated in Vence, and which was considered Matisse's masterpiece. The stained glass windows particularly pleased Marc, and he began to wonder what he might do in that medium. The seed was being planted for the masterly works that he would one day create.

It was at this time, too, that Marc discovered the magic of Monet. He felt that it was Monet who had grasped the truth about color and that his paintings had "some of the most amazing pigment." "Color should be as penetrating as walking on a thick carpet," Marc asserted. Picasso referred to Chagall as "the greatest living colorist."

Living in the south of France, Marc was now able to reestablish contact with the publisher Pierre Tériade, with whom he had been friendly before the war. At Ida's urging, Tériade had purchased her father's three great engraved works from Vollard's heirs, and now Tériade embarked upon the huge project of publishing the books. They developed a warm and happy relationship.

By now Marc Chagall was sixty-three years old, but he still moved with the grace of a dancer, and his elfin smile and blue eyes radiated energy. He had a secret shyness, and was only totally at ease with his family and closest friends. But everyone felt at ease with him. His incredibly mobile face was constantly changing from earnestness to unexpected clowning, from comic to lightning intelligence. Often, in the middle of a conversation, a pensive shadow would fall across his face, he would stop talking, and he would leave abruptly. His imaginative world had overtaken him. A sudden idea had sent him hurrying into his studio.

About eighty percent of his day was devoted to work: collecting impressions, sketching, painting, meeting people in the art world, and visiting museums. He began early, stopping for an hour's walk before lunch. Then he worked all afternoon until dinner.

"You must work a lot; it clears the brain," he advised young painters.

He was strong and healthy, but his only exercise was his daily walk. Habitually dressed in baggy trousers, checked shirt, and a shapeless sweater, he would walk along sniffing the breeze and swaying slightly in rhythm to the tune he was humming. "This is the way I used to wander the streets of Vitebsk," he reminisced.

As he walked through the alleys and town squares of the old walled quarter of Vence, watching the children at play there, he would suddenly open his sketchbook and begin to draw. But it was not these children he was sketching. It was a memory of his own childhood, triggered by these present-day youngsters. The world of his childhood remained always in a chosen corner of his heart. "You cannot walk among children without remembering your own childhood," he commented.

There was always the possibility that what he was looking at then would also become part of his memory bank of images and be sketched at a future time. "My pictures are painted collections of inner images which possess me," he explained. "I am unable to see how I draw. My hand sees, but my eyes are often turned toward the interior and focused on other drawings and paintings I shall realize one day." His sketchbooks were records of the past and sources for the future.

Back at work in his studio, Marc would first sketch in the broad lines with charcoal, then lay out the colors. Sometimes he would borrow unexpected colored objects to hold against the canvas to see the effect. Virginia learned to look for missing items in his pile of treasures. Once he even took brightly colored socks from the children's room.

His restless hands moved quickly as he drew, but he worked patiently on very small sections, and the painting grew slowly. Often he worked on the same canvas for weeks or even months. He always had several paintings in progress at the same time.

In 1951 Ida helped organize a large exhibition of her father's work in Jerusalem, and Marc was invited to attend. It would be his first return to the area since the State of Israel had been created as the Jewish homeland in 1948. This time he invited Virginia to accompany him, but she was hesitant to accept. She had never attended one of his openings. She understood that Marc wanted her to play the role that Bella would have played, and she was uneasy. She disliked large official functions, and she felt unworthy.

But she did go, and everyone who met her loved her. The trip was a triumph for her as well as for Marc. With his tall, sweet, lovely Virginia at his side, Marc was received almost as a conqueror.

On their return to Vence, Marc was fired with a new enthusiasm. He started several very large paintings of scenes from the Old Testament, including *Moses Receiv-*

ing the Tablets of the Law, *Moses Breaking the Tablets of the Law*, and *The Crossing of the Red Sea*.

Virginia began to feel that she and Marc were drifting more and more apart. They longed for a simple life, but fame and riches made it increasingly impossible. Marc Chagall was becoming an institution, and his renown was casting a shadow over their personal relationship. It seemed to Virginia that Marc was filling his canvases with all the love and tenderness that she craved. Virginia continued to love him very much, but she couldn't play the role of Wife of the Famous Artist. She was, as always, extremely supportive of him, but she wanted to pursue her own interests as well. Marc objected. Virginia felt, too, that Marc considered his public life more important than their private life together.

Soon, Ida announced that she planed to marry Franz Meyer, a handsome young art scholar who would become director of the Künsthalle Museum in Basel, Switzerland. She then asked her father when he planned to marry Virginia. Marc, who had always glorified the institution of marriage, replied, "A quoi bon?" ("What's the point of it?"). Years later Virginia speculated that the difference in their religions meant more to him than she had imagined.

Virginia had played a vital role in Marc's recovery after Bella's death. Her youth, her beauty, her intelligence, her devotion had served to revive him. Now their separation was almost inevitable. She went out of his life as quietly as she had come into it.

12

A Prayer in Brightly Colored Glass

Once again Ida was faced with the task of caring for her heartbroken father. Immediately she began searching for someone to keep him company. Soon she learned of a divorced woman named Valentina Brodsky. She was forty years old and came from a wealthy Russian-Jewish family that had been reduced to poverty by the revolution. Valentina was living now in London, where she had a millinery business. She agreed at once to come to Vence to act as Marc's housekeeper, but on the condition that she was guaranteed marriage to the great artist.

Several months later, on July 12, 1952, Marc Chagall and Valentina Brodsky, a coolly elegant, intelligent, and cultured lady with dark hair pulled back severely from her face, were married. At the time, Marc confessed to several friends that he had no desire to marry. But after several months Valentina had helped to repair his shattered ego and had made herself so necessary that he wanted her to stay. From then on Vava, as Marc came to call her, became the dominating influence of his life.

Vava was socially ambitious and very much concerned with money matters, and she soon took over all the practical aspects of Marc's life. Along the way she systematically erased as much of her husband's past as was possible. Bella could not be erased. But Virginia could be, and even, to some extent, David, Marc's child by Virginia. Marc saw less and less of him as he grew older. And Vava brought to an end many of Marc's old friendships. Letters and phone calls went unanswered. She saw to it that even Ida no longer held the important place in her father's life that she had before Vava's arrival. In fact, six years after their marriage, when there was a conflict between Ida and her stepmother, Marc and Vava divorced and immediately remarried under a marriage contract more favorable to Vava.

But Marc was impressed with her background and with her ability, and he was happy with her. Vava, in turn, became his faithful companion, organizing his life and creating a calm atmosphere in which he was free to work. They began to divide their time between their home in Vence and a beautiful apartment in Paris. In the period immediately after their marriage Marc produced an entire series of joyous Paris paintings.

When Marc was asked by Tériade to illustrate the poem *Daphnis and Chloe*, he and Vava decided to visit Greece "in order to touch the earth behind the poem— to live in the same atmosphere and light as the characters I was going to illustrate." In Greece he found the same brilliant Mediterranean light that had so entranced him in Israel, and on his return to Vence he executed a series of lithographs drenched in color.

For the past two years Marc had been studying lithography again. He understood that there was always something for him to learn. Even at the age of sixty-five, when many people consider themselves ready to retire, Marc Chagall was learning new techniques and was about to embark on entirely new ventures.

Marc had for many years been yearning to "do a wall," to enlarge the scope of his painting. And he had been intrigued by the possibility of decorating a church, as Matisse had done. Just a few days before his marriage to Vava he had gone to see the magnificent stained glass windows of the Cathedral of Chartres, studying them carefully from the outside as well as the inside. He was moved by the brilliance of their color, particularly the blue so like the blue in his own palette. And he was delighted to discover a thoroughly Chagallian green donkey in one of the medieval medallions.

Then, in 1956, an offer was made to him to decorate a little Dominican church in the French Alps at Assy. Other artists, among them Rouault, Matisse, Braque, Lipchitz, and Leger, had also been asked to contribute to this project. Marc agonized over whether to accept. Would it make him less of a Jew to work in a church, he wondered? Would he betray his Jewish heritage? It wasn't until 1957 that he finally created two small stained glass windows, his first attempt in this medium. He used a technique known as *grisaille*, by which he delicately painted his designs in shades of one color directly onto the glass. It was a simple beginning, but it opened a new world for him.

Soon Marc was invited by the chief architect for the restoration of the great Gothic cathedral in Metz to create a cycle of large stained glass windows. By the spring of 1958 he had completed two drawings based on earlier biblical paintings, among them *Moses Receiving the Tablets of the Law.*

In order to translate these designs into glass, Marc now began his great collaboration with Charles Marq, a master glassmaker from the famous Simon workshop in Reims, just north of Paris. Marc took David along with him on his first visit to the studio, and David recalls the amazement with which Charles Marq and his wife, Brigitte Simon, watched his father at work. Struggling to work out the complex color variations of his designs, Marc learned from the Marqs the theory and technique of stained and leaded glass in only fifteen days. Marc Chagall had finally discovered the perfect medium to express his religious sense: light and color coming from within. "I *had* to make stained glass windows. I had to get myself into daylight," he explained. He was beginning to sense the vast possibilities still to come.

When Marc completed the first windows for the Metz Cathedral in 1959, they were taken from the studio to Paris, to be exhibited there. The president of Hadassah (an American Jewish women's organization) and the architect of the new Hadassah-Hebrew University Medical Center in Jerusalem came to Paris to see them. They were so impressed that they invited Chagall to create a cycle of twelve windows for the synagogue that would be a part of the hospital.

Marc was overjoyed. For the first time, he was being asked by Jews to create for Jews. At long last he would be doing something for the Jewish people, for Israel, for a synagogue.

"Why did you wait so long?" he asked them playfully. But, touched deeply, he accepted the commission immediately and temporarily set aside his work for Metz.

The terrible years of World War II, and with it the persecution of the Jews, had intensified in Marc his strong sense of being a Jew, and now he threw himself into this task with all the fervor and emotion of his soul.

"The synagogue shall be a crown for the Jewish queen and the windows the jewels of this crown. The light of heaven is in these windows and by this means they are part of the good God," he said.

They decided that the windows would symbolize the twelve tribes of Israel who were blessed by Jacob and Moses in the celebrated lyric verses that conclude Genesis and Deuteronomy.

The number twelve has many associations, among them the twelve signs of the zodiac, which are associated, in turn, with the twelve tribes of Israel, the gates of Jerusalem, and the instructions given by Moses in the book of Exodus for Aaron's "breastplate of judgment" to be inlaid with twelve brilliantly colored precious stones: *"And the stones shall be the names of the children of Israel, twelve, according to their names. . . ."*

Since Jewish law forbids the representation of the human face, which is considered an image of God, Chagall decided to turn this restriction to his advantage. He created a kingdom out of stars, elements, and animals that were the emblems of the twelve tribes and that had always been part of his imagery. And he used the symbols of Judaism—the Torah scroll, the shofar, the Star of

David, the menorah, and Hebrew letters—to portray passages in the Bible.

He didn't attempt to translate into stained glass all the images he found in the Bible. His intention was not to illustrate them in a conventional way. Rather, he wanted them to convey a sense of the mystery and spirituality of the Jewish people. It would be *his* poetic vision.

Working closely together, the Marqs and Chagall visited Jerusalem to test the intensity of the light that would flow through the windows. Back in France, they developed a special process that would allow Chagall to use three colors on a pane of glass, giving him greater freedom than the traditional technique of separating each colored pane by strips of lead. He studied, he sketched, he tested. Once again, he was learning, and he was breaking new ground.

Each morning he would enter the studio punctually, and with great humility, he would say to Charles Marq, "Now show me what you know how to do. . . ." Then, before the dazzled eyes of the workers, Marc would begin to paint on the glass that they had prepared for him.

"He looks, moves away, rejects, begins again, going mysteriously towards a new image that he does not yet know. And in this ceaseless back and forth movement, a window is born," Charles Marq described it.

For seven months, from the beginning of October, 1960, through the end of April, 1961, Chagall kept the same hours and submitted to the same rules and discipline as the craftsmen in the studio with whom he worked on equal footing. They loved him for his high standards and his kindness.

It has been said of the Jerusalem Windows that they are a prayer in brightly colored glass, that their essence lies in their color and in Chagall's magic ability to give life to material and transform it into light.

Each window has a certain dominant color to produce the effect that Chagall wanted to achieve. They form four groups of three, on each side of the building, each group having a different color—red, blue, yellow, and green. His choice of colors was guided by the instructions for making Aaron's breastplate.

As the sun moves throughout the day, its changing light pierces the work, so the windows change in intensity and hue. "The light [in the stained glass] is the light of the sky. It is that light that gives the color," Chagall explained.

In only two years the twelve large windows were completed. The little stone synagogue, set into a slope in the Judaean Hills just west of Jerusalem, was consecrated in February, 1962. Before they were installed, the windows were exhibited in the courtyard of the Louvre, in Paris, in June of 1961. The following winter they were shown at the Museum of Modern Art in New York.

"'All the time I was working, I felt my mother and father were looking over my shoulder.'"

Hundreds of thousands of people went to see them. They were Marc Chagall's gift to the people of Israel. He would accept no payment for them.

"All the time I was working [on the windows] I felt my mother and father were looking over my shoulder. And behind them were Jews—millions of other vanished Jews of yesterday and a thousand years ago," Chagall said.

In the Jerusalem Windows, because of the sacred nature of the task and the special character of stained glass, his work reached its highest peak. He had revitalized the art of the stained glass window.

Five years later, during the three weeks of tension that preceded the Six-Day War of 1967, the Israelis began to fear the possibility of damage to the windows. When they cabled Chagall to ask him how they might protect them, his immediate answer was, "You worry about the war. I'll take care of the windows. If there is any damage to the windows, I'll replace them with even nicer ones."

On Monday morning the war began, and a bomb fell into the reflecting pool outside the synagogue. The shrapnell which flew up did, indeed, damage three windows. Later Chagall repaired them beautifully. But he left a hole in one of them. His reasons were threefold: First, he cited the Jewish tradition that to recall the destruction of the Temple of Jerusalem, a small section of a house should be left unfinished; second, the hole would serve as a memorial of the war; and third, he said impishly, the value of the window would increase substantially because of the human story behind it.

Now Chagall returned, exultant, to his interrupted

work for the Metz Cathedral, completing the windows for it in 1968. Here he created not only biblical themes, but delicate floral designs as well. His joy and love of nature shine through these windows.

He was recognized now as the great master of the twentieth century. He created stained glass windows for churches in England and Switzerland, for the Rockefeller family Union Church of Pocantico Hills in Tarrytown, New York, and for the United Nations Building, in memory of Dag Hammarskjold, former United Nations Secretary General, who had died in 1961.

Commissions for the "monumental" works that he had hoped for continued to arrive from all over the world, and were to be executed in still new media. Perhaps most important in his eyes was the request to decorate Israel's new Knesset building, which would house the first parliament in the history of the Jewish nation. For Marc Chagall it was the culmination of his lifelong "romance" with Judaism. It became for him a labor of love, and once again he refused payment. This would be his gift to the Jewish people and to Israel.

Deciding that tapestries would be the most appropriate decoration for the gallery wall, he designed *Exodus, Entry Into Jerusalem,* and *Isaiah's Prophecy,* expressing in these three huge panels the history of his people and its focal points, the land of Israel and Jerusalem, the city of David. His designs were executed by the highly regarded Gobelins Tapestry Manufacturers. Caught up in the excitement of the project, he added more and more to his gift. Using stones from the Negev, he created twelve floor mosaics and a wall mosaic entitled *The Western Wall.*

13

Painting a Dream

"A day can come in the life of a painter when his genius explodes and leads him to sum up his entire life in a picture. That's what happened to Chagall with the opera ceiling." So said André Malraux, French Minister of Culture, at the end of July, 1964.

Five years before, in 1959, when Malraux became Minister of Culture, he began bringing new vigor into the cultural life in France. Then, in 1962, hoping to revitalize the ornate, century-old Paris Opera House, he asked Chagall to create new ceiling decorations for the vast circular dome of the auditorium.

Chagall was troubled by the request "because I am afraid of commissions, though inwardly I dream of monumental works," yet he was "touched and deeply moved by the confidence and vision of Malraux."

The ceiling, from which hangs a huge crystal chan-

delier, presented a great technical challenge. But perhaps an even greater obstacle was the fact that almost
everybody in the French art world seemed to be unhappy with the choice of Marc Chagall. What right,
they asked, did a modern artist have to tamper with an
historic monument? And why was such an important
project being given to a "foreigner"?

Chagall was uneasy for a long time. "I had doubts
about myself, about my work . . . I doubted day and
night." But all the problems seemed only to stimulate
his fantastic imagination and his desire to meet the challenge. So when Vava said, "Try to do a few rough
sketches and you'll see," he slowly began to compose
circular drawings. He would accept no payment for his
work, he decided. He would make this a gift to his
adopted country.

He thought of the opera house as a whole, conscious
always of its architecture and of the design of the original ceiling, which he diplomatically decided to leave in-
tact a few inches above his. As he studied the area, he
decided that he wanted it to reflect, "as though in a mir-
ror high above, in a bouquet of dreams, the creations of
actors and musicians, and to keep in mind that down
below the colors of the clothing of the audience were
moving about." He wanted it "to sing like a bird, without theory or method; to pay homage to the great composers of operas and ballets. What is sometimes called
unthinkable is possible," he said. "Our dreams are only
thirsty for love." He would breathe life back into this
building, he vowed to himself.

He began with pastel sketches the size of dinner
plates, then large sketches which he transferred onto
canvas. To cover the 2,153-square-foot circle, he used

four hundred and forty pounds of paint. Standing atop a seventy-foot scaffold, wearing a white housepainter's coat, with music from *The Magic Flute* or a Mozart symphony playing in the background, the seventy-seven-year-old Marc Chagall applied every bit by his own hand. In fact, he often used his finger instead of a brush to massage color into the work.

He conceived of the whole design as a flower with five petals, each with a dominant color to represent particular composers, and each to contain figures and symbols from the world of ballet and opera. Mozart would occupy half of the blue section, which would contain angels and a bird playing *The Magic Flute*. Moussorgsky, whom Chagall considered the father of Russian music, would fill the rest of the blue space. He would portray dancers from Adam's *Giselle* and Tchaikovsky's *Swan Lake* in yellow. Stravinsky's *Firebird* and Ravel's *Daphnis and Chloe* would be honored in the red petal. Debussy's *Pelleas and Melisande* would appear in the white petal, set off by yellow. Finally, two more pairs of lovers, Berlioz' *Romeo and Juliet* and Wagner's *Tristan and Isolde*, would be portrayed in the green panel. Although the inner circle around the chandelier had originally been left empty, Chagall chose to paint it with references to works by Gluck, Bizet, Verdi, and Beethoven. And, just as painters had done in the past when they wished to honor their patrons, Chagall decided to paint in the face of André Malraux.

He made many studies and sketches, taking great care in determining the areas of color and then the designs to be used. Always, he painted with flowers next to his palette to remind him of the "chemistry" of colors in nature. And he repainted every square foot of the canvas at least once to get it just the way he envisioned it, intensifying his colors right up to the last minute.

Often Vava came to sit quietly by and watch him at work. His grandchildren, Ida's son, Piet, and her twin daughters, Bella and Meret, came, too.

Then, on September 23, 1964, more than two thousand invited guests sat expectantly in the darkened auditorium of the opera house. A performance of *Daphnis and Chloe*, for which Marc had designed costumes and sets, was about to start. The ceiling was not visible. The music began and the entire corps de ballet began to dance. As the dancers reached the front of the stage, the great chandelier was lit and Marc Chagall's soaring canopy burst into bloom, casting its magic spell. There was a moment of hushed silence, then thunderous applause as all eyes turned toward the box at the rear where a beaming Marc Chagall acknowledged their acclaim. Once again, he had done the impossible. He had painted his dream.

14

A Message of Faith

At the age of seventy-seven, Chagall was beginning to find the twenty-one step spiral staircase leading to his studio difficult to manage several times a day. Then, when a building was erected near Les Collines that blocked his view and made it possible from the new building for people to see into his garden with binoculars, he and Vava decided that they had no choice but to move from Vence. "My landscape was mutilated. I was sick at heart," he said.

They chose the adjacent town of St. Paul de Vence, a quiet and welcoming town that looks from a distance like a stone ship that has run aground on a hilltop. They loved its tranquil atmosphere and its narrow, winding streets paved with cobblestones that preserved the original look of a walled medieval city. Here, in a wooded park above the village, facing the mountains, they built a large, sprawling Provençal house of local stone with a red tiled roof. It was completed in July of 1966, and when they moved in they named it La Colline. From here Chagall could walk to the Maeght Foundation whenever he liked or wander into the village to watch a game of *pétanque,* the "national" sport of Provence.

Under Vava's supervision everything in the house was designed to facilitate her husband's work. Three studios were built—two for painting and one for engraving. The largest even had a moveable wall that could be raised or lowered automatically to avoid the need to climb up on scaffolding to work on large compositions. An elevator was installed between the studio and the bedroom. Marc Chagall had come a long way from his young artist days at La Ruche.

But he never forgot his roots. And he never forgot his Bella. "She was all love, only love," he wrote of her to a friend in Israel in 1969, on the twenty-fifth anniversary of her death. He loved Vava, but in a different way.

She provided the companionship he needed to survive. He called her the *guidon* of his life, for she brought order and harmony into his existence. It was she who would interrupt a conversation with a friend to remind her husband of another appointment. And it was she who checked to see that he had money in his pocket to pay for a taxi cab.

But she was never able to bring order into his studio. Since his days at La Ruche, he had always worked amidst clutter. Everywhere in his studio there were racks of canvases and dozens of palettes filled with dried paint. Books on art, birds, and flowers were piled on tables. Photographs of relatives and postcards of great paintings were tacked to the walls. A phonograph was always playing one of the dozens of classical records of his favorite composers that were stacked up. And always there was a bubbling samovar. His sketchbooks, too, filled with rough ideas for compositions, color notes, observations, sometimes even remarks written in Russian, were piled up here. This was his private world, and no one entered without an invitation.

Everywhere in the house were fresh flowers. The minute they began to fade he would prod Vava to replace them.

By now Marc Chagall's yearning to "do a wall" must certainly have been satisfied. At just about this time, however, quietly and without fanfare, he accepted yet another commission for a monumental task. He created two enormous murals (36′×30′) entitled *The Sources of Music* and *The Triumph of Music*, to hang in the windows of New York City's new Metropolitan Opera House overlooking Lincoln Center Plaza. Once again, Marc Chagall was paying tribute to the great composers of the past, particularly his beloved Mozart. These magnificent canvas panels—one predominantly red, the other yellow—add color and warmth to the area just above the lobby entrance. Viewed through the windows from outside, they appear almost like stained glass.

Then, just a short time later, on February 19, 1967, Mozart's *The Magic Flute*, an opera of childlike magic and delight that mirrored Chagall's own sense of fantasy, opened there. He had designed the more than seventy-five costumes and thirteen sets.

Marc Chagall's greatest triumph and the one closest to his heart was yet to come. When he had first settled in Vence back in 1950, there was near his house an abandoned chapel. For a long time he had hoped that he would be asked to decorate it.

Often he would stand alone in the silence of the little church, measuring each wall, judging the light, and contemplating the empty white spaces. Then he would allow his imagination to take over, carrying him back to his childhood visions of the world of the Bible, to the legends Uncle Neuch had read to him, and to his memories of Vitebsk. As powerful images appeared in his head, he could almost hear the stories of the Bible like the sound of golden music. The idea of a series of religious paintings was beginning to take shape—a series of poetic variations on biblical themes.

Back in his studio, he would plunge into work, bringing his vision of these stories to life on canvas. By 1955 he had painted seventeen majestic pictures in brilliant color with themes from Genesis, Exodus, and The Song of Songs. These works became the crowning glory of all the studies he had been doing for so many years. But at that time he was not asked to do the project for the church, and he set the paintings aside.

Now, more than ten years later, he returned to these works, adding to the seventeen oil paintings the thirty-nine gouaches he had done in Palestine back in 1931, three sculptures, drawings, and the engraved *Bible* published by Tériade. When he completed the series in 1967 he called it the *Biblical Message*.

As he reflected on the fact that the true spiritual starting point of these works went all the way back to his first stay in Palestine, Chagall decided that he would present the series as a gift to the State of Israel, which he always referred to as *Unser Land* (Our Land). But the forceful Vava objected. The series should remain in France, she felt. So Chagall offered it to the French government instead. Twenty-three years later, in the spring of 1990, Ida would compensate for this loss to Israel by donating 103 works of art by her father from her own collection to the Israel Museum in Jerusalem.

Now, André Malraux, accepting this splendid gift to France, made an equally splendid gesture. The series would be exhibited in the Louvre, an honor never before accorded a living painter. "Life is more fantastic than dreams!" the overwhelmed Marc Chagall exclaimed when he was informed of the decision. Three hundred thousand visitors came to see the exhibit during the summer of 1967.

Then Malraux made an even more spectacular gesture. A museum would be built in Cimiez, high on a hill above Nice, with the light of the Mediterranean Sea to nourish it, to house the exhibit permanently. It would be called *Le Musée National Message Biblique Marc Chagall* and would be the only national museum in France devoted to a living artist. The first stone, taken from the neighboring mountains, was laid in 1969. The completed building was dedicated on July 7, 1973, Marc Chagall's eighty-sixth birthday.

Its collection includes the *Biblical Message* as well as all the biblical illustrations originally done for Vollard, additional lithographs of biblical scenes, a tapestry woven for the entrance that displays a vast Judean landscape under two blazing suns, a monumental mosaic in the back courtyard depicting *The Prophet Elijah*, and three breathtaking stained glass windows called *The Creation* in the music and lecture room. Their blue reminds one of the blue of Chartres. In fact, when Chagall was asked, in front of these windows, why the color blue was so prominent in his work, he answered, "Why blue? Because I am blue, just as Rembrandt was brown."

The building is not simply a museum. Marc Chagall envisioned it as a place where all people "could find a certain peace, a certain spirituality, a religious feeling, a feeling of life. To my mind," he said, "these paintings do not represent the dream of a single people but of all mankind." His was a message for people of all faiths, in the hope of fostering human understanding, peace, and love.

"Perhaps young people and the not-so-young will come into this House seeking an ideal of brotherhood and love such as my colors and lines have dreamed. Perhaps someone will utter here the words of love I feel for all. Perhaps there will be no more enemies and . . . the young and not-so-young will build a world of love out of new colors. . . . In art, as in life, all is possible when conceived in love."

"The Bible has fascinated me since childhood," he wrote in the preface to the catalogue of the museum. "I have always thought of it as the greatest source of poetry of all times. I have sought its reflection in life and in art."

In moments of doubt the greatness and wisdom of its poetry soothed him. And he believed that if people were to read carefully the words of the prophets, they would find in them the keys to life. As he painted the Bible, it became an album of portraits of one of the greatest families of mankind. Today the people of the Old Testament come to life for us and live in our memory. His pictures inspire us to hurry to read what the people in the Bible said.

It was now more than fifty years since Marc Chagall had last left Russia, and he longed to return. After several preliminary trips there by Ida to pave the way, he was finally invited by the Soviet Minister of Culture to a special exhibition of a few of his works. For years Chagall had been trying, unsuccessfully, to convince the Soviet authorities to exhibit some of his early work that had been locked up in vaults there for decades.

Now he and Vava made an emotional trip back to his homeland, traveling to Moscow and Leningrad, the former St. Petersburg, where he was reunited with two of his sisters. His mother and his other sisters had likely perished in the Nazi invasion of Vitebsk in June, 1941.

As a surprise, three of the murals he had painted for the Jewish State Theatre in Moscow so many years before were spread out on the floor for him to see. There were tears in his eyes as he signed them.

There was much criticism of this trip because it came at a time when anti-Semitism was strong in Russia, and Soviet authorities were making it impossible for Jews to emigrate to Israel. In spite of this, and even as a Jew, Chagall retained a deep love of his homeland. But he refused to visit Vitebsk. Little remained of the town he had known as a child. Most of it had been burned to the ground by the Nazis during the Holocaust. Miraculously, Chagall's house still stands.

It wasn't until many years later, in the spring of 1991, with the help of the new cultural freedom in Russia, that the remaining murals were exhibited in an art gallery in Switzerland. They had lain rolled and crumpled in the basement of Moscow's Tretyakov Museum for seventy years. Now the Russian government had finally agreed to allow them to leave the country. The ceiling and the curtains from the theater are still missing.

Art historians, viewing the murals for the first time, proclaimed them the best work Chagall had ever done. Several contain the original versions of paintings that have long hung in museums. In fact, the murals were called "*the* major work of Jewish cultural value in the plastic arts in the 20th century." But Marc Chagall did not live to hear this.

In the last years of his life Marc Chagall continued to fulfill commissions for monumental works all over the world, and to garner awards—from universities, from royalty, from presidents—too numerous to list. He would beam happily as a child as he showed them to friends.

He was the first Jewish artist for whom the doors of

"Sometimes in fine weather he painted outdoors."

the great European cathedrals were opened. When he accepted an invitation to create the windows for the Cathedral of Reims, the national church of France, a commission he had long dreamed of receiving, many Jews accused him of having "converted." His rueful reply to his critics was, "What a kovet [honor] for a Jew from Vitebsk to make the windows in the cathedral where French kings were crowned." He completed these windows when he was eighty-seven years old.

He had moved away from the easel to the wall, accepting with energy and excitement the challenge of new art forms and monumental scale that few artists have ever been offered. But his basic "vocabulary" that he had developed by the mid 1920s remained the same. In his painting the same vigor, freshness, and youthfulness remained. "The sign of a masterpiece is its freshness," he counseled young artists. "One must struggle, struggle, struggle, and then perhaps we'll win out.

He continued to paint his dreams of love and joy every day, beginning early in the morning. His work was his life, and perhaps it was his work that prolonged his life, for he lived to be ninety-seven. "The day I stop working I will die," he told his friends.

Sometimes in fine weather he painted outdoors. In the garden, filled with the sounds of humming insects and the songs of the birds, he would set his canvas against a tree trunk near the flower beds to see "if my painting holds up in nature. If it doesn't disturb the harmony," he said, "then it is real, and perhaps one day I could put my name to it."

His belief in himself was unshakable, and his seemingly limitless energy and self-confidence gave him the resilience he needed to survive life's trials. As he found fulfillment in his work and in those he loved, he showed us a rich vision of life's possibilities. He tried his hand at every medium—painting, lithography, sculpture, ceramics, mosaics, stained glass, tapestry, and decoration—all with dazzling results. He was able to take from every school of art what he needed, and then go his own way, but his individualism obliged him to make his life experiences into pictures. His paintings became his biography: "If my art played no role in the life of my family, they, on the other hand, greatly influenced my art."

He took great pride in his granddaughter, Bella's namesake. They spent many happy hours together when she was a young art history student in Paris, often walking hand-in-hand, always laughing a lot. He encouraged her and hung a painting of hers in a prominent place in his house. "He made me feel alive," she said.

At the beginning of the spring of 1985, Chagall's health appeared to be failing. For the first time he was unable to accept an invitation to attend a major exhibition of his work at the Philadelphia Museum of Art. The news spread that Chagall was not well.

Bella, visiting him then, described him as looking very small in his bed, "like an angel."

Since he had settled in the south of France, Marc Chagall had been a member of the small community of Ashkenazik Jews in Nice, and he had become a good friend of the rabbi of Temple Israélite and the Chief Rabbi of Nice, as well as the Chief Rabbi of France. When they heard that Chagall was ill, they phoned and asked for permission to visit him. Vava Chagall refused.

Then, on the evening of March 28, 1985, as he was being taken by elevator in his wheelchair from his studio to his bedroom, simply and quietly, and with a faint smile on his lips, Marc Chagall closed his eyes for the last time.

When the rabbis learned from a radio broadcast that Marc Chagall had died, they telephoned once again to offer a burial plot in the Jewish cemetery in Nice. Vava refused even to take their calls.

David, too, heard of his father's death secondhand. His mother had heard the news on a radio broadcast early the next morning and had phoned David to tell him.

The only cemetery in St. Paul de Vence is a very small Roman Catholic one where only longtime residents of the village have the right of burial. But once again Vava's forcefulness asserted itself. Determined that her husband would not be buried in a Jewish cemetery, she used much influence with the mayor of St. Paul to obtain a plot.

The day of the funeral dawned bright and beautiful. A gladdening spring sun shone over the little cemetery,

transformed now into a dazzling garden of flowers. Hundreds of people were gathered from around the world. David stood quietly in the background during the short but moving ceremony. Nothing was said to indicate that Marc Chagall, whose Judaism had been such a vital part of his life and whose paintings shine with an inner light of Judaism, had even been a Jew. Then, just as the casket was being lowered into the ground, a friend standing with David stepped forward and recited the Kaddish, the Jewish prayer for the dead.

GLOSSARY OF ART TERMS

cubism A movement in art in which the artists imagined the objects, figures, and even landscapes they were painting to be made up of geometric shapes and painted them as though seen from many different angles. Pablo Picasso and Georges Braque developed this style of painting.

engraving A form of graphic art in which a design is cut into a copper plate with a steel tool. The plate is then inked and run through a press where the image is transferred to paper, producing a print.

etching A form of graphic art in which a design is scratched with a needle onto a wax-coated copper plate. The plate is then bathed in an acid that etches (bites) the lines into the copper.

Expressionist A school of art in which artists use colors and shapes to express their feelings.

Fauves A group of Expressionist painters working chiefly in France who liked violent colors and often changed the shape of the things they painted. Because of this, they became known as the "Fauves" (wild beasts). Henri Matisse was their leader.

gouache   Painting done with an opaque watercolor prepared with gum.

grisaille   A style of painting in shades of gray.

Impressionists   A group of painters who were more interested in capturing momentary effects of light and atmosphere than subject matter. They achieved this through their use of color applied in small dashes, which blend in the observer's eye. They painted mainly outdoors.

lithography   A printing process in which the image to be printed is drawn on a flat surface such as stone, then treated to retain ink, while the background areas repel the ink.

mosaic   A technique in which small pieces of colored glass, stone, or other materials are inlaid in a background material to form a design.

pigment   A dry, powdered substance that when mixed with a suitable liquid, gives color to paint.

woodcut   A print made from a piece of wood upon which a design has been carved. (It is the oldest pictorial printing technique.)

IMPORTANT DATES

1887	Marc Chagall is born in Vitebsk, Russia, on July 7.
1900	Completes studies at cheder; is enrolled in public elementary school.
1905	Wave of pogroms begins in Russia.
1906	Enrolls in Jehuda Pen's School of Painting.
1907	Goes to St. Petersburg to study art.
1908	Begins to study art with Leon Bakst.
1909	Meets and falls in love with Bella Rosenfeld.
1910	Goes to Paris to study art; comes in contact with work of the French masters and with revolutionary new movements in art.
1911	Moves into studio in La Ruche; meets other émigré artists.
1913	Paints *Paris Through the Window, I and the Village*.
1914	Is introduced to Herwath Walden, who exhibits Chagall's work in *Der Sturm*, his gallery in Berlin.

	Travels there for opening, then continues on to Vitebsk and reunion with Bella.
	World War I begins.
	Paints almost sixty "documents" of Vitebsk, including *Praying Jew*.
1915	Paints *The Birthday* on July 7.
	Marries Bella on July 25.
1916	Their daughter, Ida, is born.
1917	October Revolution in Russia takes place.
	Chagall paints *Promenade, Double Portrait with Wine Glass, Above the City,* and *Cemetery Gates*.
	Begins writing his memoirs.
1918	World War I ends.
	Is appointed Commissar of Fine Arts for Vitebsk; organizes festivities to commemorate October Revolution.
1920	Moves to Moscow with Bella and Ida; designs murals, sets, and costumes for Jewish Theatre.
1921	Leaves Russia; goes to Berlin in May; studies graphic art with Hermann Struck; etchings to illustrate *My Life* are published.
1923	With Bella and Ida, returns to Paris September 1. Meets Ambroise Vollard, who commissions him to illustrate Gogol's *Dead Souls*.
	Begins to travel in France with Bella and Ida.
1926	Has first exhibition of his paintings in New York City.
1927	Is commissioned by Vollard to do series of circus paintings.
1928–31	Illustrates the *Fables* of La Fontaine.
1929	*Ma Vie* published in French.
1930	Is asked by Vollard to do series of illustrations for the Bible.
1931	Travels to Palestine with Bella and Ida.
1932	Travels to Holland with Bella and Ida.
1933	Retrospective exhibition of his work is held at Künsthalle in Basel, Switzerland. Chagall is rec-

ognized as one of the great artists of the twentieth century.

1934   Ida is married to Michel Gorday. Chagall paints *Bride's Armchair* in celebration.

Travels to Spain with Bella.

1935   Travels to Poland with Bella.

1937   Becomes French citizen.

1939   Completes sixty-six plates for *The Bible*. Vollard dies.

Germans invade Poland on September 1; World War II is officially declared.

Chagall paints *White Crucifixion*. Is awarded Carnegie Prize.

1940   Chagalls move to the south of France.

Chagalls escape from France; arrive in New York on June 23.

Chagall's work exhibited regularly at Galérie Pierre Matisse.

1942   Commissioned by Ballet Theater to design scenery and costumes for ballet *Aleko*.

Premiere on September 8 of *Aleko* in Mexico City.

1944   Paris is liberated on August 25.

Bella dies suddenly in Cranberry Lake, New York, on September 2. Chagall stops painting for nine months.

1945   Chagall meets Virginia Haggard.

Accepts commission to design settings and costumes for ballet *Firebird*.

1946   Moves to High Falls, New York, with Virginia.

Begins illustrations for *One Thousand and One Nights*.

Has exhibition of his paintings at Museum of Modern Art in New York in April.

Travels to Paris for opening of exhibition of his work at Musée d'Art Moderne in May.

His son, David, is born June 22.

1948	Returns to France with Virginia and David in August and settles in Orgeval, near Paris.
	Dead Souls published by Tériade.
1950	Moves to Vence. There he often meets Picasso and Matisse, who live nearby.
	Aimé Maeght becomes his exclusive dealer.
	Completes many paintings of flowers and tries his hand at pottery making.
	Reestablishes contact with the publisher Pierre Tériade.
1951	Travels to Israel for large exhibition of his work.
	Begins work on very large paintings of scenes from the Old Testament, which ultimately become his *Biblical Message*.
1952	Ida marries Franz Meyer in January.
	Virginia leaves Chagall in March.
	Chagall marries Valentina Brodsky on July 12. They travel to Greece in preparation for his illustrations of the poem *Daphnis and Chloe*.
	Chagall resumes the study of lithography and resumes work on illustrations for *The Bible*.
	Fables of La Fontaine published by Tériade.
1956	Completes entire series of *Bible* illustrations (105 etchings).
	Chagall's *Bible* published by Tériade.
1957	Creates two small stained glass windows for Dominican Church at Assy.
	Exhibition of his engraved works at Bibliothèque Nationale, Paris.
1958	Completes designs for stained glass windows of Cathedral of Metz.
	Begins collaboration with master glassmaker, Charles Marq.
1959	Exhibition of Metz Cathedral windows in Paris.
	Is invited to create cycle of twelve windows for the synagogue of the Hadassah–Hebrew University Medical Center in Jerusalem.

1960	Receives honorary degree from Brandeis University, Waltham, Massachusetts.
1961	Completes Hadassah windows. They are exhibited in courtyard of the Louvre, in Paris, in June, and later, at Museum of Modern Art in New York.
1962	Hadassah windows installed and synagogue consecrated in February.
1964	Unveiling of his *Peace* windows at United Nations Building in New York.
	Unveiling on September 23 of his newly designed ceiling for Paris Opera House at performance of the ballet *Daphnis and Chloe*, for which he had designed costumes and sets.
1966	Moves to St. Paul de Vence in July.
	Creates two murals for opening of Metropolitan Opera House in New York.
1967	*Biblical Message* series exhibited at the Louvre.
1968	Completes work on windows for Metz Cathedral.
1969	Building begins on Musée National Message Biblique Marc Chagall, Nice, the only national museum in France devoted to a living artist.
	Travels to Jerusalem for opening of new Knesset building and unveiling of his tapestries and mosaics there.
1973	With his wife, Vava, travels to Moscow and Leningrad for exhibition of his work. Is reunited with two of his sisters.
	Musée National Message Biblique Marc Chagall is inaugurated on July 7, his birthday.
1974	Unveiling of his *Four Seasons*, a huge outdoor mosaic, in Chicago.
	Consecration on June 14 of his windows in the apse of the Cathedral of Reims, the national church of his adopted country.
1974–85	Continues to create stained glass windows for other monumental public works all over the world.

Receives many awards and honorary degrees.

1977   Is made honorary citizen of Jerusalem.

Is awarded Grand Cross of the Legion of Honor.

1985   Major exhibition of his work held at Philadelphia Museum of Art, which he is unable to attend because of failing health.

Dies on March 28 at his home in St. Paul de Vence.

INDEX

WORKS BY MARC CHAGALL

mentioned in the text

Books Illustrated by Marc Chagall